FUSION

CHILDREN'S MINISTRY

BOOK TWO: FAMILY, SCIENCE, STRATEGY

Created by the Northwest Ministry Network:
Brent Colby, Annie Bailey, Monica Bowsher, Nick Caalim,
Jessica Downs, Dorene Heeter, Amy Johnson, Dan
Metteer, Bryan Reeder, Chantel Rohr, Kate Thaete

To Les:

Thank you for believing in children's ministries.

Our churches and communities are forever changed because of your willingness to do the things that God called you to do.

TABLE OF CONTENTS

INTRODUCTION

fu·sion /ˈfyo͞oZHən

The process or result of joining two or more
things together to form a single entity.

SUCCESSFUL CHILDREN'S MINISTRY

What makes a children's ministry successful? I put this question to
dozens leaders across the Pacific Northwest and came up with a list.
A team of leaders helped me refine these "big ideas" into a series of
essential starting points for you and your children's ministry. I
listened to these experienced leaders and became inspired. I knew
that we had to capture their thoughts and share them with you. The
Fusion Children's Ministry Series is a collaborative project designed
to capture and share the best ideas about kid ministry. The authors
of these chapters may not be considered *gurus,* but they are experts
in their field. They are successful pastors leading out of a local
church one week at a time. They serve all types of families in all
types of places. Weather you have a large or small church, budget,
team, or facility this book is for you.

HOW THE SERIES WORKS

The Fusion Children's Ministry Series includes more than
thirty big ideas about children's ministry. These ideas have been
spread out over three books which focus on the themes of theology,
leadership, culture, family, science, strategy, history, environments,
and pastoral ministry. That may sound like a lot of themes, and you

are right. Our goal is to share from our own experiences, which are both deep and wide. The Fusion Children's Ministry Series is designed to be a starting point for you and your team. We don't have all the answers, but we have some excellent ideas and even better questions.

This is the second book in the Fusion Children's Ministry Series and will cover the topics of family, science, and strategy. Family includes ideas around ministering to the kid in the context of siblings, parents, and other family members. Science examines childhood development and thought processes to help you be a more effective teacher. Strategy picks up a few nuts and bolts of children's ministry and lays them out on the table. You will notice that we build off of Book One which discussed the topics of theology, leadership, and culture. If you haven't checked out that text I suggest you do. Chronology is not important but the content is.

You Got This

So what makes a successful children's ministry? You do, God does, and so does your team. We want this book encourage you, challenge you, and make you a better leader. Don't read it alone! Invite some other people in your church to read it with you and discuss the ideas in each chapter. The reflection questions at the end of each chapter are designed for you to answer with others.

Enough standing around here in the introduction. Let's kick this thing off with part four and some ideas surrounding family ministry.

PART FOUR: FAMILY

Family describes the role that the ministry plays at home. The children's pastor plays a support role to the parent and, while this support may be extensive, it will always be secondary. We will discuss how to balance the idea of family and children's ministry in your church and on your team. There is a lot of confusion about the two terms and if they actually make a difference when practiced in the local church. Our second idea focuses on the very practical subject of hosting a parent meeting. The third chapter is built around the idea of helping parents disciple children. What are you waiting for? Turn the page!

4.1 BALANCING CHILDREN AND FAMILY MINISTRY
Kate Thaete

When Jesus called me into ministry, it felt like He forgot to tell me what He intended for me to do. I knew at age eighteen that I was supposed to pursue full-time ministry, but it took five more years to have any idea whatsoever of what I'd be doing. Not really liking other people's kids (and not having any of my own, so for all I knew, not liking kids at all), I was recruited for children's ministry. And after a solid year of serving there, Jesus had changed my heart—and was giving me a job.

While I lived out this newfound love for kids and deep desire to see them loving Jesus, I recognized a deeper love for families. A child of divorce, I cared greatly about strong marriages. Not growing up in a Christian home, I was desperate to see parents involved in their children's faith, but had no real experience. And so about six years after my foray into the world of children's ministry, my role began to unfold and transition into Family Ministries. I'd love to tell you that, two years in, I have it all figured out, but I don't. It's like making a suit. There's so much drafting, basting, trying it on, not liking one part but loving another, and tailoring it to fit perfectly. But I have learned a few things about the differences between family ministries and children's ministries, and how and when they work together. I've also had to wrestle with how the family minister does children's ministry—because if I thought the family ministry role would immediately lead to my exit from children's ministry involvement, I was naive. The last two years have shown me that, if anything, family ministry is not a departure from children's ministry, but simply the other side of the same coin.

Defining Family Ministry

There seem to be many interpretations of what family ministry should look like. Since there's no cut-and-dried biblical model for this, only loose guidelines, it seems that Jesus wants us to have the freedom to minister to families in ways that suit our culture and context. In America in the past ten years, there have developed as many ways of doing family ministry as there are churches. But there seem to be a few strategies that churches are gravitating toward more and more.

A common trend has been for churches to issue the "Family Pastor" title as a broad-scope role under which they could lump together children's programming, youth programming, and events geared toward married people and the whole family. Sounds busy, doesn't it? It is. It's not a stretch to imagine how leadership would get to this conclusion: if a church already has an effective children's minister, why wouldn't they also bring effectiveness to other struggling or lacking ministry areas? But this path seems like a surefire road to burnout for the children's ministry leader and very likely even the highest-capacity volunteers around them.

In other scenarios, churches use family ministry to create a series of family-oriented events, believing that what the family needs most is to spend more quality time together, focused around Jesus. This method adds to what is universally an already-packed family schedule, and teaches families to be dependent on the church for their spiritual growth, both as individuals and as families. This is a dangerous method that at its worst could develop a generation more dependent upon the church (and less dependent on Jesus himself) than any generation past.

And somewhere, in the deep recesses of their thought processes, tired children's ministers think, if we embrace family ministry, we can stop doing children's ministry, and then I'll only have to plan twelve events a year, instead of fifty-two.

Let's talk more about that idea. When is a family ministry strategy so effective that the children's ministry becomes superfluous?

Never.

A BICYCLE MADE FOR TWO

Family ministry and children's ministry need each other, because the whole they create together is greater than the sum of the two parts. Think of the tandem bicycle. You might think of this two-seated bicycle as only a regular bike with room for an extra rider, but there's a unique strategy that comes with riding a tandem bicycle. In order for anyone to get anywhere, both riders need to understand and master this strategy.

A tandem cycling team is made up of a "captain" (the front seat) and a "stoker" (the back seat). The two seats offer a completely different perspective: the stoker cannot see the road ahead, whereas the captain has a full view. Each rider has a different job as well. The captain's major responsibility is to control the bike, its balance, steering, shifting and braking—and to communicate well with his stoker. In doing so, the captain earns his stoker's trust, without which it would be impossible for the stoker to do his job effectively without impeding on the captain's responsibilities. The stoker is the motor of the bicycle. Because he doesn't need to concern himself with bike control, he can focus on generating power. But really, the stoker's major responsibility is to not steer. A simple shift of his weight could negate the work of the captain, or worse, tip the bike completely.[1]

You can see that learning to ride in tandem is not a leisurely afternoon activity. Neither is finding the synthesis of the family pastor and children's ministry. It takes hours of practice for the two roles to learn how to work well together, to communicate and anticipate. It takes learning, trust, and a clear understanding of differences, roles, and responsibilities.

In a well-strategized world, the family pastor should serve as the captain. They have the full view of the road ahead, and they know where they should be going. They carry the vision. The children's ministry is a partner in this, not serving a different vision, but the same. Because direction has already been determined, the children's ministry can put all of its effort into moving that vision forward. For the two to work together requires strategy, communication, and trust.

There is a danger in creating a series of family-oriented events and calling that your family ministry strategy. You're simply creating another program. Who has time for that? Instead, it seems like the most effective family ministry efforts are when we let family ministry influence the way we minister to children and youth. Every children's ministry and youth ministry effort is judged by its value for equipping parents to pastor their children and partnering with the family in a child's faith development.

So when do we do away with children's ministry? We don't. Family ministry and children's ministry are heading for the same destination, from two different perspectives. When they work together, each carrying out their responsibilities, their contribution to the effort, they allow a church to reach that destination more quickly. A strong children's ministry gives kids an experience that reinforces God's love for them. Leaders who are invested in the lives of kids are saying the same things at church that parents are saying at home. A strong children's ministry teaches kids that church is a safe place to ask questions, to build relationships, and to find acceptance—no matter what they're struggling with. Meanwhile, family ministry equips parents to be their children's primary pastors, so that Jesus is more than just a Sunday activity, and parents are leading the charge on faith development at home.

CHILDREN AND FAMILY MINISTRY

Whatever family ministry looks like in your context, make sure that children's ministry is a part of that picture, and not a separate picture altogether. You'll find that your efforts are more effective when the two are working in tandem.

REFLECTION QUESTIONS

1. What has been your perspective on the relationship between family ministries and children's ministries?
2. What has been your church's or church leadership's perspective on the relationship between family ministries and children's ministries?
3. What would it look like for children's ministry and family ministry to work in tandem in your church?
4. What two or three simple changes could you make to bring your children's ministry and family ministry into better alignment?

END OF CHAPTER NOTES

[1] Sheldon Brown, "Tandem Bicycles," Cycling Blog, Harris Cyclery, , http://www.sheldonbrown.com/tandem.html (accessed October 2, 2015).

4.2 HOSTING YOUR NEXT PARENT MEETING
Dan Metteer

I was twenty-one years old when I began serving as a children's pastor. Twenty-one! I was barely past ordering off the kids' menu, and now I was supposed to be giving spiritual guidance to families. I did my best to act grown-up, but most of the time it was faking it. And there were several occasions when my cover was blown.

After I had been at my church for a few months, a concerned mother approached me for some pastoral advice. "Pastor Dan," she said cautiously, "my six-year-old daughter has been asking some specific questions, and, well…um…when is it the right time to talk to your children about sex?" I froze. I was stunned (although I was proud of myself that at least I did not giggle when she said the word "sex.").

I stumbled through a vague, deflecting answer, I walked away wondering, "Why would she ask *me*? I don't even have kids! I don't know the first thing about talking to kids about sex."

That day I learned an important principle: When you lead in children's ministry, parents want to hear what you have to say.

Your Voice Matters

One of the wonderful things about children's ministry is that it provides opportunities for people who are young and/or new to ministry to serve the church. But the scary thing is that these young and/or inexperienced people are being handed one of the most important and impactful ministries of the church.

Recently, I spoke to a class of college students who were preparing to lead in children's ministry. Explaining that they would soon be in a position where they would have to speak into the lives of not just kids, but also parents, I asked the students to raise their hand if they felt ready to speak to parents as peers. Exactly zero hands went up.

It can be overwhelming to lead people who lead their own kids, whether you have children of your own or not. But if you have been given a position of leadership within the children's ministry of the church, then three things are true:

You are an influencer to kids.
You are an influencer to parents.
Your influence will impact eternity.

Your voice matters. If you are leading in ministry, then God has entrusted you with carrying the plan to move his mission forward. Parents need to hear that plan, see what it looks like, and get as excited about it as you are, so that the church and the home can partner together.

Also, here is a little secret about parenting: parents do not have all of the answers about parenting. They need help. And *you* can offer tools to assist with the most important part of parenting—raising kids to love Jesus.

BENEFITS OF THE PARENT MEETING

If you are able to have a sit-down, face-to-face with every parent in your church every year, then great! You are probably doing a great job of letting your voice be heard, and establishing a rapport with them. But if that isn't going to fit into your schedule, then an annual parent meeting is the answer.

If your ministry does not include an annual meeting where parents are invited to come together and hear your heart, what your ministry is about, and how the church and the family can partner together, then it's time to get one on the calendar! A parent meeting can increase your influence as a leader to parents as well as kids. It can take your goals and values for your ministry off a paper and put them in the hearts of families. It can build enthusiasm and participation for your ministry's programs, events, and initiatives. And it will stretch you as a leader.

One word of warning here—you may be thinking, "Wow, if having a parent meeting can do all of these great things, why not have one more than once a year? How about every quarter? Or every month?" While every church culture is different, and meeting more often than once per year might work in your situation, it is probably not a great idea. The kind of meeting we are talking about here should be special. You and your leadership team should put in hours of work to prepare for it, and it should be eagerly anticipated by the parents who attend. Once (or maybe twice) per year is probably just right.

WHAT SHOULD BE INCLUDED

The agenda for this meeting should be intentional and strategic. So be sure that you actually have a clear agenda! This is no time to shoot from the hip. Include the right things:

Mission and vision. If parents don't understand what your ministry is trying to do or how that mission is going to be done, then they will likely be frustrated. But if they have a clear understanding of your ministry's mission and your vision for seeing that mission done, then they can be excited with you. Communicate your mission and vision clearly, and with passion! Let your parent meeting stoke the fire for parents to be your ministry's biggest supporters. If you don't have a clear mission or vision, then get one! Pray about it, dream with your team, and let God speak to you until you are able to communicate that mission and vision to others.

Values and culture. Your ministry's values should determine its culture and the "how" for everything you do. The parent meeting is a great time to establish some expectations. If you value safety, and you can articulate why it is important, the parents will be much more patient next time they have to wait in line to check in their kids, or get their pick-up tag checked. If you are trying to establish a culture where kids bring their Bibles to church, and you let the parents know about it, they can try to make sure the kids grab their Bibles before leaving the house. If your ministry is based around family devotions done at home, letting parents know about the plan and purpose for this can set their expectation so you can see success, instead of frustration, in your values and goals.

Overview of your ministry program. This may seem unbelievable to you, but it is true: Most parents do not have a clear idea of everything your church does to minister to children. They might not know about the midweek program or Bible memory reward system. They might not know about student leadership opportunities for their kids or about the family service projects they could do. They have maybe never heard about the kids' worship team or the incentives to invite friends to church. And even if your ministry does only one or two of these things, it is likely that the parents do not have a clear idea about what really goes on in those programs.

Don't take forever to explain every little detail, but give your parents a clear idea about what they can involve their kids with and why it is important.

Important dates. I am a dad of three kids. One thing I am noticing, as my kids get older, is how difficult it is to manage the schedules of five different people. But we can plan around just about anything—birthday parties, school fundraisers, sports, and church events—if we know about them in *advance.*

Let your parents know what is coming up in the next year that their kids will want to (or be expected to) be a part of, how much it is going to cost, and what kind of time commitment it will take. It will build their trust in your leadership, and make for some much happier parents.

Volunteer opportunities. Hopefully, involving parents as volunteers in your ministry is something you want to do. If so, talk about it at the parent meeting. This is your chance to look them in the eye, and tell them with all sincerity that they should serve for the good of the church, their kids, and themselves. This is your chance to put aside gimmicks and recruiting tactics, and invite parents to serve Jesus. If the parents have heard your heart, and have felt your passion, it should be an easy invitation.

WHAT SHOULDN'T BE INCLUDED

A pastor once told me, "People won't remember what you said, but they will remember how they felt when you said it." Of course, I *did* remember what that pastor said . . . so I guess there are some exceptions. Anyway, the point is that feelings are more important than information. As you communicate with the parents, be sure to leave out some of these parent meeting no-nos:

Technical difficulties. If you have a video or song that perfectly captures the message you want communicate, but you can't get it to play or the sound won't work, then that's what you call a "backfire." It will work against you more than it was ever going to work for you. It will sap the energy out of your meeting, and you will be left trying to carry on through your own flop sweat. Practice the video cues ahead of time, or just keep it simple and stay within your technical comfort level.

Excuses. There are, of course, a lot of things you *could* include in this meeting. But explaining that you *were* going to have a calendar of events, or the printed materials were *supposed* to be in color just underscores the message that you are disorganized. Ditch the excuses, and focus on what you've got.

Boredom. Again, there are a lot of things that you could do in this meeting. But keep it moving. Make it fun. If you work with kids, then you know how to keep attention. Just make sure you don't forget those principles when you talk to the adults. Use visuals, break up information into bite-sized chunks, and have fun. No one needs another boring meeting.

The All-Important "When?"

Holding your meeting at the wrong time can make all of your hard work be for nothing. Being strategic about when the meeting will occur is one of the most important decisions you can make. There is no perfect time, but there are definitely wrong times to have it. For example, Christmas Eve or the Fourth of July are not great days to do it. Those are ridiculous examples, but it underscores the point that there are bad days to try to coordinate a gathering. Avoid weekends when there is already a big women's event, a missions dinner, or something else that is going to require extra time at church. If possible, give at least a couple of weeks between big events and your meeting.

Also, look for times when parents are in a natural mindset of family improvement and health. My favorite months for new initiatives are September (after school starts), January (after Christmas and the beginning of the new year), and May (just as parents start to think about summer changes). Your church may have a month that works even better. The point is to be *strategic.*

Getting Parents to Come

While parents *do* want to hear from you, they also have busy schedules and different priorities to maintain. It's important to do all you can to get parents to come to the parents' meeting. Small attendance can make for a disappointing meeting for you, and it could send the message to the parents who did come that the meeting was not important.

Spread the word early. If you invite parents to a meeting that is happening tomorrow, you will not only get a sparse crowd, but you will send the message that you are not a well-organized leader. Put your next meeting on the calendar several weeks or months in advance, and let parents know so they can put it on their calendars.

Utilize influencers. There are a few parents in your church that just about everybody will listen to. Maybe it is a board member, the pastor's wife, or just the mom or dad everybody loves. Getting that person to not just come, but to be talking about the meeting will make a big difference. How do you get that person to do that? You could assign that person a role at the meeting (like a short training), get them involved in the planning of the meeting agenda, or simply just *ask* them to be there.

Make it meaningful. If all you do at your meeting is transfer information, smart parents will just figure out how to get the notes later. But if you offer the parents the opportunity to let their voices be heard—maybe by letting them have input for your VBS dates, or deciding what kind of prizes are given out in your kids church—they will feel valued and will be glad they came!

Remember they are PARENTS. One complication that you are almost certainly going to face is childcare. They are parents, after all. Every one of them has kids. There are several solutions to this problem. Find one that works for you. Get teenage volunteers to watch the kids, pay some single adults, work out a childcare trade with the church across town, or put on a movie for the kids in the room across the hall. Just make sure you plan for this issue, and let the parents know you have a solution.

If you feed them, they will come. This is a tried-and-true method for luring people to meetings! Food is a great motivator. If you are able to serve a meal (like a lunch after church, or a weeknight dinner), the meeting can actually *save* parents time, since they won't have to prepare a meal for the family. But even if you just offer some snacks, it will increase the likelihood people will come, and it will make the mood of the meeting feel relaxed and enjoyable.

YOU WERE MEANT FOR THIS

In thinking about getting up in front of every parent in your church and speaking to them about all of these things, you may be asking yourself, "Can I really do this?" The answer is Yes! And how do I know? Because God has positioned you where you are doing what you are doing for a reason. You are part of the body of Christ, gifted by the Holy Spirit to do what he has called you to do. Put in the work, put in the prayer, but lead with confidence. You've got this!

REFLECTION QUESTIONS

1. If you could wave a magic wand and get every parent in your church to do one thing, what would it be? What is the next step you could take to make that a reality?

2. What person or group would the parents in your church really benefit by hearing from? How can you get that person at your parent meeting?

3. What Scripture speaks most clearly to you about the importance of ministry to children? How can you plant that verse in the hearts of the parents in your church?

4.3 HELPING PARENTS DISCIPLE CHILDREN
Bryan Reeder

As a parent to three great kids I was never fully prepared to disciple, train, teach, and cultivate them spiritually. I certainly didn't take that class at Bible College! So many things in life are sink or swim.

Parenting is the hardest job that I have ever had. There's that pressure to be proficient in so many areas: math, sports, braiding hair.

One of my favorite things to do with my kids is to play sports with them. As a child, I dreamed of being the next Magic Johnson or Michael Jordan or Tiger Woods. My dreams ended sometime in middle school when it became readily apparent that I was way too short, too slow, and too uncoordinated to ever be a professional athlete. I am very thankful that my kids enjoy sports (even though my daughter sinned by choosing soccer over softball).

Becoming a great athlete starts with some natural ability but it also takes a great deal of work. Michael Jordan was cut from his high school basketball team as a freshman. He didn't start great. It took a whole lot of training to make him great. Training our kids spiritually is very similar. God created us as spiritual beings. But just as it takes work to develop your athletic abilities, it takes work to grow spiritually.

For many parents, myself included, it's easier to go play catch with their son than to tell him a story from the Bible. I enjoy both of those things but the latter is more challenging. I don't think I'm alone in this. Many parents struggle with being the spiritual leader in their home.

Most parents want to spend time with their kids. They have good intentions about talking to their kids on a deeper level. They want to share their faith. The problem is—they don't know how. A survey of parents by the Barna Group notes that close to nine out of ten parents of children under age thirteen believe they have the primary responsibility for teaching their children about religious beliefs and spiritual matters. However, a majority of parents do not spend any time during a typical week discussing religious materials with their children. Instead they generally rely on their church to do all of the religious training their children will receive. In the book, *Transforming Children into Spiritual Champions,* author George Barna says that "Parents are not unwilling to provide spiritual leadership for their children, but they are ill-equipped to lead them in this way."[2]

While church is important, God designed the family to be the primary place where discipleship happens. So the church's job is to come alongside families and help them fulfill the instructions given in Deuteronomy. The Bible clearly teaches that parents are to spiritually train their children or to lead in the provision of spiritual development for their children:

> Hear, O Israel: The Lord our God, the Lord
> is One. Love the Lord your God with all your heart
> and with all your soul and with all your strength.
> These commandments that I give you today are to
> be upon your hearts. Impress them on your children.
> Talk about them when you sit at home and when
> you walk along the road, when you lie down and
> when you get up. Tie them as symbols on your
> hands and bind them on your foreheads. Write them
> on doorframes of your houses and on your gates.
> (Deuteronomy 6:4–9, NIV)

I want to share with you some key elements in preparing parents to be the spiritual leaders of their home. This might be our most important role as children's pastors and leaders. As Proverbs 22:6 (NIV) says, "Start children off on the way they should go, and even when they are old they will not turn from it."

DEVELOP A CULTURE

There's a lot of discussion today about culture. Culture can be defined as the prevailing attitudes which dictate actions, behaviors and habits. Culture is simply how we do things. Unfortunately, few churches and children's and family ministries create culture on purpose. It just happens or evolves over time. For me the first element in partnering with parents in spiritually training their children is to develop that culture.

I lived in Grants Pass, Oregon for about ten years. Grants Pass is the home of Dutch Bros. Coffee. (You may have seen them profiled on the television show, *Undercover Boss.*) There are now Dutch Bros. Coffee stands in several states. Every stand I have been to, and I have been to several, has a similar culture. If you visit one and you should, you will notice the energetic and young broistas (yes, they call them broistas instead of baristas), loud music, sweet coffee, kid-friendly atmosphere, and terrific customer service. Their distinct culture is established even before a broista is hired. It begins during the interview process. The culture at Dutch Bros. is just as important as the coffee they sell.

Your children's and family ministry culture isn't as important as the message of the gospel, but it is crucial if you want to partner with parents as the primary spiritual leaders. Partnering with parents in spiritual training is not another program, but rather it needs to become a part of your church's culture. Reggie Joiner in his book, Think Orange, suggests, "Family ministry should not be another program you add to your list of programs. It should be the filter you use to create and evaluate what you do to influence children and teenagers."[3]

To create the culture of partnering with parents you have to do something about it. Changing culture will require a shift in thinking, a shift in priorities, and a shift in calendar. Actions speak louder than words. Simply stating that parents are the primarily spiritual leaders is a good start, but it doesn't change the culture.

Some beginning steps you may want to consider would be preaching a sermon or a sermon series on partnering with parents, or offering a life group on spiritual parenting, or hosting a parent meeting or workshop.

A year or so ago I hosted a parent meeting. It wasn't a meeting about events or just to distribute information. Rather it was a purposeful gathering to begin the process of creating a culture of partnering with parents.

REACTIVATE THE FAMILY

Part of the goal of creating a culture that emphasizes partnering with parents is about engaging or reactivating the family. Reactivate means to restore the ability to function or the effectiveness of something.

I am not good with my hands. No one ever calls me to help with a home remodel or car repair. I'm thankful for friends who have helped me numerous times. Over the years I have encountered several issues with a car battery. If my battery is dead, so is my car. I can turn the key again and again and again, but if the battery is lifeless nothing is going to happen. My car has lost its effectiveness to function.

Changing the culture and reactivating the family may require a new battery or a new sense of urgency. Many of our families are inactive and are just going through the motions. The average regular church attender only comes three out of eight Sundays. Most parents fit one of these following categories:[4]

Uninterested: Parents are indifferent about a particular situation or development.

Aware: Parents are concerned about a particular situation or development. These parents are outside the church, but open to it, and they're interested in becoming better parents.

Involved: Parents have a basic or entry-level relationship with the church. Even if it's just bringing their kids to church, these parents are taking steps to influence kids spiritually.

Engaged: Parents are committed to partnering with the church. They are growing in their relationships with God and assume some responsibility for spiritual leadership in the home.

Invested: Parents proactively devote time and energy to partnering with the church. They understand the strategy of the church's ministry and are in community with Christian parent groups.

It would be notable if the uninterested parent could become the invested parent overnight. It would also be outstanding if I joined the PGA tour tomorrow. Neither is likely to happen. A more realistic goal is to take it one step at a time. The key is finding ways to get parents involved so they move from being an uninterested parent to (eventually) an invested parent.

Dick Gruber, the children's ministry professor at Valley Forge Christian College, suggests several ways for reactivating the family:[5]

- Establish parental visits in children's programming. "Parent of the week."
- Enlist parent in entry-level ministry with their children. When asked, many parents will refuse the weekly commitment to serve. Those same parents do not mind serving once in a while for a big event.
- Engage parents in the decision-making process. You may want to gather a group of leaders and parents on a regular schedule to give input or make decisions for the children of your church.

Sometimes getting a parent involved is more about what they get out of it then what they do for you in regard to serving. The goal of having a parent serve is not so they can fill a spot but so they can eventually become an invested parent.

There are many stories I could share about one parent who started out at one of the first two levels (uninterested, aware), but then began to get involved, thus starting a gradual process of moving towards being an invested parent.

SERVE AS A RESOURCE TO FAMILIES

An element that works alongside creating a culture and reactivating the family is enriching parents through resourcing them. The church must serve as a resource to parents. This can include a reading list to help parents through every stage of their child's life, a lending library of books, and seminars for parents. Above all, be available.

Today there are so many quality children's and family ministry resources that help parents. For me, that's one of the top priorities when choosing a curriculum. I wouldn't use a curriculum today that didn't have some sort of family devotion or resource for parents.

Each month we create a monthly parent packet that provides parents resources to help them to be the spiritual leaders in their homes. These simple resources help parts to start a conversation about spiritual matters. There are suggestions for different activities in family life from mealtime to bedtime to drive time. The point is to use everyday situations for parents to lead their kids spiritually. In the parent packets we include daily devotions for kids as well.

It's also important to me to provide these resources digitally. I don't know about your kids and your parents, but in my situation families tend to "forget" to take the packets home or they tend to be left somewhere at church. So these resources are available on our church website as well.

Social media is a great tool to connect with parents as well outside of a Sunday morning. Start a Facebook page or a group for your posts. Get on Instagram. Tweet out reminders about the resources provided in the monthly parent packet.

PROVIDE SHARED EXPERIENCES

Creating a culture of partnering with parents is not only about reactivating the family and providing resources, but it can also extend to providing opportunities for families to worship or serve together. Providing shared spiritual growth experiences that parents can participate in can help reactivate the family; this moves them toward being invested parents.

Consider creating special events such as a shared worship experience, a father-son campout, a daddy-daughter night, a family camp, etc. These experiences can be catalyst for getting parents involved in their child's spiritual life.

We have hosted several "Family Xperiences" over the years. This is simply an opportunity to bring parents and kids together. I have done these events once a month and once a quarter. Just do them. They can be anywhere from fifteen to forty-five minutes long. It's a great way for families to worship together and to introduce to the entire family what is being taught at church.

CLOSING SUMMARY

Children's pastor Ryan Frank often states that "The shift from children's ministry to family ministry is probably the biggest trend in children's ministry today." While you attempt to partner with parents, don't forget that the church still needs children's pastors, too. Kids still need you.

As you work with your teams to create a shift in your culture keep in mind that it is a process and will require time to get where you want to go. Look for opportunities to celebrate little wins and to recognize milestones in the lives of families. Your effort in changing culture may be one of your most important tasks.

REFLECTION QUESTIONS

1. What is your church culture? Does it say anything about parents and church leaders working together?
2. Why do you believe families and churches are in need of a cultural shift?
3. Of these five, where do most of your parents land? (1) Uninterested, (2) Aware, (3) Involved, (4) Engaged, (5) Invested. Where could an uninterested parent serve that would help him or her progress toward being an invested parent?
4. How are you currently providing resources for your families? Is it effective? What improvements need to be made?
5. What shared worship experience or serving opportunity can you offer as part of your partnership with parents?
6. If a parent asked you where to begin, what advice would you give him or her?

Bryan Reeder

END OF CHAPTER NOTES

[2] George Barna and Bill Hybels, *Transforming Children into Spiritual Champions* (Grand Rapids, Mich.: Baker, 2003).

[3] Reggie Joiner, *Think Orange: Imagine the Impact When Church and Family Collide. . .* (Colorado Springs: David C. Cook, 2009).

[4] Joiner, p. 163.

[5] Dick Gruber, [Podcast] "Partnering with Parents, Internships | DickGruber.com," http://www.dickgruber.com/podcast-partnering-with-parents-internships/ (accessed October 2, 2015).

4.4 INTRODUCING: MILLENNIALS AS PARENTS
Annie Bailey and Brent Colby

The Millennials are the most studied generation to date and everybody has something to say about them. Pundits from the world of technology, business, and education recognize the great potential of these young men and women; they are creative, hardworking, and socially aware. But the same critics foster reservations about a generation with limited perspective, idealistic dreams, and inflated egos. Church leaders are also concerned about reaching this generation of young men and women as fewer of them attend church or are interested in religious spirituality. And as the years go on, something important is beginning to take place: members of this once youthful, headstrong generation are now the grown-ups, and they're starting to have children of their own. Come along with us as we examine this unique generation. Let's find out who they are and how our ministries can prepare to welcome them, and their children, into our churches.

This chapter will paint a clear picture of the Millennials attending your church. We will describe how to have the greatest effect over these young parents and address issues of authenticity, tolerance, community, leadership, and technology.

LOOKING BACK

We are talking about generational trends of those born between the 1980 and 2000. Previous generations include groups like the Builders, Boomers, and Generation X. Each of these shares a range of characteristics which have been influenced by political, economic, or technological trends. By examining shared values, behaviors, and beliefs we can begin to understand what is most important to them, how to spur them toward action, and how to influence their world view.

THE AMERICAN FAMILY: A WALK DOWN MEMORY LANE

Prior to the 1960s, parents believed that it was their responsibility to lead the educational, spiritual, and moral development of their children. It was, for the most part, a partnership with the church and schools. There wasn't a significant need in the church to develop many resources for children to learn about God as children sat in church with the adults and children and parents took the lead in their children's spiritual formation. In the first half of the nineteenth century we lived in a culturally Christian nation, where church attendance and spiritual growth were valued.

Many parts of American culture changed after the mid-century, and ideas surrounding faith and family began to change with the times as well. Among Baby Boomer parents, those born 1946–1964, independence from organized religion began, divorce rates rose, busyness and social disconnectedness increased, while religious philosophies and family structures changed. As a result, many overwhelmed, isolated, and religiously disconnected parents began to abdicate traditional roles of moral and spiritual authority. These parents surrendered their responsibilities to the local church and looked to religious leaders for the Christian formation of their kids. Ministry leader positions and resources were created to reach their children, known as Generation X (1965–1979), but many adopted a postmodern and secular view of the world. In response, the church doubled down on its efforts to reach a generation.

During this time, Baby Boomer parents began to return to the church, and many Gen-Xers responded to the gospel and started to raise families of their own. Kids, born between the years of 1980 and 2000 grew up in a world very different from any previous generation. With the influence of Gen-X and Baby Boomer parents and a world inoculated with technology, Millennials saw things from an entirely unique perspective. As children, they were studied as by-products of previous generations, and much was predicted about them during their adolescent years. But if you look across the landscape of the church today, you will realize that something profound has begun to change: the Millennial generation is having kids of their own and are reclaiming the role of spiritual leader that their parents and grandparents once relinquished.

SNAPSHOT OF THE MILLENNIAL

The characteristics and needs of the Millennial generation are vastly different from prior generations. Ministry leaders must recognize *why* these adults are different and *how* to reach them as young mothers and fathers. Their unique needs, increased numbers, and postmodern cultural influences sound a clarion call for ministry leaders to consider a more effective approach to engage them in their churches. The Millennial generation derives its name from being the first generation to come of age in the new millennium. They are the children of Baby Boomer and early Gen-X children.[6] They make up one-third of the population in the United States, and are considered the most influential generation since the Builder generation of World War II. Their childhood experiences are based on an overly-busy, fast-paced, and ever-changing society, which renders them extremely adaptable to change. They are smart—the most educated generation yet—civic-minded, and morally tolerant. Their family values differ from previous generations as well. Millennials are getting married later than generations before them—the average age for men is twenty-nine and for women twenty-seven, which is up from the average of twenty-three and twenty in the 1960s. Many are in committed relationships, however, with almost 10 percent cohabitating before marriage and 24 percent buying a home with their significant other before marriage.[7] While many do not consider marriage a significant marker of adulthood, they do care strongly about parenting. According to Pew Research, when asked what was one of the most important things in their lives, only one-third said that having a successful marriage was the most important thing, while 52 percent gave this designation to being a good parent.[8]

Now that we have a better picture of this generation, let's focus on ways to engage them by examining five characteristics that have the greatest impact on the church. We want each of these characteristics to change the way you think about young parents in your ministry today. The following are some potential responses, but don't interpret our suggestions as the final word. You know your church and are in the best position to find ways to reach this generation of young parents.

NEED FOR AUTHENTICITY

One of the most significant characteristics of Millennials is their need for authenticity: the ability to express individuality and have "real" interactions with others. Tattoos, fashion, art, and social media are all mediums for modern expression of authenticity. For previous generations, tattoos were taboo; they were the mark of the sailor and rebel. For Millennials, however, tattoos are a form of art and self-expression, and more than one-third of Millennials have them.[9] Their need for authenticity also emerges in social and organizational interactions. Millennials are known for having built-in radars for "fake" or posturing behavior, and will shy away from people or organizations perceived as being inauthentic. In an attempt to relate to Millennials, many Baby Boomer leaders have made the unfortunate mistake of sporting skinny jeans and deep v's while using phrases like "hashtag" in their sermon. These adaptations are made in the name of relevance. However Millennials are more interested in sincerity. They don't want leaders who are their brand of "cool," they want leaders who possess wisdom, live authentically, and demonstrate character.

LEAD OUT OF TRANSPARENCY

Leaders have been given great latitude to be themselves in speech, dress, and style. We are more likely to be accepted so long as we are being transparent. Transparency involves being honest about ourselves, projecting an accurate image of we are and what we believe. When we say that we can "see right through" someone, we are saying that we can assess their motives, character, and abilities with certainty. Millennials can detect a phony from miles away. Remember this: You are only qualified to be you. Don't feel obligated to act, speak, or dress like someone else.

Many young pastors feel pressured to develop a ministry persona where they use the right words, wear the right clothes, and have the right attitude. Make no mistake; popular culture will always be popular. But transparent leaders self-regulate the balance between trends and authenticity. Young parents are not looking for a personality to disciple their children; they want pastors, teachers, and leaders whom they can trust, who are caring and willing to be themselves. The concept of strengths-based leadership, popularized by Tom Rath,[10] is particularly effective with Millennials today. Become great where you are good and embrace the gifts that God has given you.

Transparency is never as easy as it sounds. Becoming a transparent leader will require each of us to confront our insecurities, ineptitudes, and idiosyncrasies. You can't be honest about yourself with others until you can be honest about yourself with yourself. There are many assessment tools designed to help you see your own strengths and weaknesses. Use them and remember that no one expects you to be perfect; but they do expect you to be improving. Transparent leadership requires great courage. You must conquer the fear of embarrassment, feelings of inferiority, and anxiety about losing church families on account of your imperfection.[11]

Millennials are likely to consider your admission of weakness as a testimony to your character.[12] Your imperfections create an ideal environment to discuss God and the Bible. They will expect their children's pastor to know the Bible and to tell the truth; but more importantly, they will expect you to be honest about what you do and don't know. Young parents want their kids to see an adult respond to

Jesus out of his or her own life and story. They expect to see the same type of authenticity in your leadership as well. An honest five-year plan will have greater effect than an impressive-sounding five-year plan. Embrace this uncertainty in your ministry and realize that constant change may be the most permanent aspect of your ministry forecast.[13] This uncertainty can't be eliminated by confidence or hard work; it can only be navigated one step at a time. Millennials are more willing to follow children's pastors who have a plan but *don't have it all figured out* so long as they are honest about what they do and do not know.

MORAL TOLERANCE AS TRUTH

Steven Covey said, "The way we see things is the source of the way we think and the way we act."[14] All world views are developed on a foundation of truth, and every decision we make is based on our beliefs. The most significant difference in generations is in this single characteristic: moral tolerance as truth. Understanding this is the foundational key to understanding Millennials. Millennials were raised to be good, moral people. This is a direct effect of postmodern thought: questioning the foundations of truth and how anything can be known for sure. As a result, the foundation of truth is pointedly different from past generations who are more likely to believe in absolute truth. In the 1990s, tolerance became the new culturally accepted "religion." Whether by their parents or by culture, Millennials were taught that truth is unknowable and morals are based on the foundation of maintaining social harmony and individualism. That is to say, *everyone has his or her own truth based on "what feels right to me."* While tolerant, it doesn't mean that Millennials don't have opinions or strong beliefs, they do. It means that *their* truth is based on their own personal experience and feelings.

While tolerance may be the defining characteristic of their belief system, the pressure and pursuit of becoming good people is a significant expectation. They have embraced it too: Millennials care for the environment and help the poor; they've revived the movement for gender equality, and have become social entrepreneurs. Many of their causes have resonated with popular culture and found great success, such as the equal rights for the LGBTQ community. In their eyes, tolerance is less about being good, and more about making the world a better place in spite of differences.

You might ask how Millennials differ from other generations who have struggled with, and even championed some of the same issues. The difference is impact. There is a metaphor that illustrates this well: Baby Boomers laid the foundation of the house, Generation X drew up the blueprints and acquired the materials, and Millennials built the house in four days while having sold it simultaneously for twice its worth.[15] Millennials have the passion, resources, and unrelenting idealism to take whatever social cause they choose to an entirely different level. For example, the Builder generation dealt with giving women the right to vote. The Baby Boomer generation advocated for women's rights on the grounds of political, social, and economic equality to men. Women's rights in the workplace were also introduced as well as a few opportunities for leadership positions. The Millennial generation, however, is not satisfied with giving women a seat at the leadership table, but is leading a gender-united charge in the fight for equal pay and leadership opportunities. Additionally, while there has been a shift over the past thirty years in how the LGBTQ community have been viewed in America, Millennials have led the charge in the significant cultural and legal shift over the past five to ten years, fighting for equal rights and the end of social exclusion. At first glance, many from older generations might misattribute the Millennials' involvement as compromise and agreement with immorality. For Millennials, homosexual rights and inclusion is not so much a fight about religion or even truth as it pertains to morality or doctrine, but about giving equal rights to human beings. Again, many Millennials may not agree with the morality of homosexuality, but that will not keep them from extending the same rights everyone else has to the marginalized.

CREATING CULTURES OF GRACE AND TRUTH

Church leaders must discover ways to create a culture of grace and truth within their ministries. According to a recent research study, 34 percent of Millennials said that they *simply don't know what makes anything morally wrong or right.*[16] While Millennials may be morally tolerant, they are not moral anarchists. There is a difference between knowing truth and recognizing truth. The relativistic nature of a postmodern world view makes it difficult for Millennials to believe that anything is absolutely true. The cornerstones of fundamentalism can crush the sensitivities of young parents today. So how do you preach absolute truth to an audience that doesn't believe it exists? It starts with this: grace.

Grace carries two powerful connotations that are important for us today. The first is biblical: grace as salvation through the forgiveness of sin. Paul writes about it in his letter to the Christians in Ephesus, "For it is by grace you have been saved, through faith - and this is not from yourselves, it is the gift of God."[17] Grace is undeserved forgiveness; the ultimate expression of justice through Jesus Christ. We are forgiven because we are loved; we are judged through the lens of Jesus' forgiveness. The second connotation is a cultural one: grace as elegance and refinement. You will find a way to influence young parents today when you approach them through the lens of forgiveness and sensitivity. Truth is a pill that can only be swallowed in this way.

Millennials will recognize, respect, and respond to a biblical moral code when it is presented in the context of grace. This does not lessen the truth of the gospel, nor does it undermine the doctrines of sin. It does, however, bridge the cultural gap that exists between traditional and Millennial worldviews.

The most effective way to install biblical truth into the life of a young family is to help them discover it. Help your families discover God's truth by setting it up for them and then letting them go off on their own adventure. Smacking someone upside the head with a Bible can work on occasion. However, you will get a better response by sending individuals out on their own collision course with the truth. Give them opportunities to read the Bible together; help them worship, give, and pray as a family. Trust that the word of God is powerful enough to change lives and be prepared to respond to questions they may have about God's story.

It's not enough to model grace and truth within the walls of your church. This approach toward culture must extend beyond the church property. If we fail to follow this pattern outside of the church then we will fail to reach Millennials as parents. Gabe Lyons urges us to become *restorers* of culture instead of allowing culture to threaten or offend us.[18] Show God's love to all people without strings attached. Serving and impacting our communities is something Millennials value. It lends credibility to our message and provides opportunity for Millennials to be a part of something they already believe in. We shouldn't hide or withdraw from popular culture no matter how dark and gloomy it may appear to be. Trust the Holy

Spirit to work through your ministry and accept the work on face value: love because He first loved us.[19] It's easy to identify the sickness in our communities and wage war against it. It is much harder to identify healthy families and campaign for their success. Speak life into your parents and allow your love for them, and your love for Christ, to drive away fear. It's important to let young parents know what it looks like to create a home life of grace and peace.[20]

SPIRITUALLY INDEPENDENT BUT RELATIONALLY DEPENDENT

Among those who were not born as Millennials, there is a common belief that Millennials are either uninterested in spirituality or they are uninterested in church. The good news is that the first belief couldn't be more wrong. The bad news is that the second couldn't be more right . . . at least for a majority of Millennials. They have confused spirituality, religion, and church organization. Spirituality is considered to be personal, even private, and the idea that God can be found in many places and forms is a prominently held view. According to the *Barna FRAME Sacred Roots Study*,[21] there were five primary reasons Millennials said they didn't attend church: I find God elsewhere, it's not relevant to me, church is boring, God is missing from the church, and church is out of date. Conversely, those who said they did go was because they wanted to be closer to God, learn about God at church, their kids learn about God there, the church does good work in the world, and because their friends were there.[22] From this we can see that there is a disconnection not from God, but from church. And for those who do attend, this gives us a glimpse into their values.

While their approach to spirituality may be private, even unconventional, their desire for community and need for close relationships is fundamental. Millennials want to discover faith on their spiritual journey, but they are more likely to do so with people they have an affinity with. Tim Elmore calls this *belonging before believing*.[23] Reinforcing this idea, Rick Richardson explains that "postmoderns are more likely to join us on a spiritual journey than to respond to a one-time, high-pressure conversion sales pitch, that they are more eager to hear the Bible's grand story than the dogmatic statements into which that story has been abstracted by theologians."[24] Ultimately, Millennials are on a spiritual journey they can't see, with people they have yet to meet, and need a faith community they don't know exists

FOSTERING CONVERSATION AND COMMUNITY

Create a place where people can belong. As pastors, we usually consider church to be a welcoming and friendly place. However, Millennials who don't go to church consider Christians to be judgmental (87%), hypocritical (85%), anti-homosexual (91%), and insensitive to others (70%). I'm sure that this doesn't reflect the reality of your church. But you should know that you are fighting an uphill battle with the average parents with young kids. In order to combat these unfair stereotypes, you must find a way to show young parents who you really are. This is what many people refer to as your church culture.

Culture is established by what you value, what you believe, and how you behave. People intuitively pick up on these things and create opinions about your ministry before they even realize it. You need to tell people what is most important to you and you need to align your actions with your words. In this way, church culture is not something that you do; it must be a reflection of who you are. This may seem as though it could be time-consuming, but when it comes to engaging Millennials, we get very few chances to get it right. We have already stressed the importance of transparency. Allowing young parents to see your beliefs in action is an essential step toward fostering a healthy, and engaging, church culture.[25]

Embracing young parents can sound easier than it really is. Millennials will bring a multitude of challenges to the table. Be prepared support adults who are entering into a needy and vulnerable phase of life. For most adults, having a child will be the most difficult thing they have ever done. Their careers, marriages, and identities are at risk. Many parents enter into a critical "make or break" phase when kids enter the mix. It becomes your job, as a pastor, to communicate a vision for their family that challenges them to become better husbands, better wives, and better parents.

Encourage Millennials to speak openly about their challenges. They are just beginning to understand parenthood, so let's create a culture of safety and openness for parents who are struggling or having questions. You will help facilitate close bonds between parents when they are encouraged to speak openly and honestly with each other. We don't believe that you need to schedule a ton of parent events. Rather, be intentional about the spaces and times that you do have. Think *environment* over *event.* It can be tempting, and dangerous, to over-program the family calendar.[26] Many churches in the 90s prided themselves on how many nights a week their church was open for events and activities. Resist the urge to dominate the family schedule. And make sure that everyone on your team goes out of their way to welcome anyone and everyone who shows up to connect.[27]

LEADERS AS FACILITATORS AND IMPLEMENTERS

One of the characteristics of Millennials is that they want "authentic" leadership. This expectation flows from their need for authenticity in all areas of life. Gone are the days where authoritarian, image-controlled leadership was effective and respected—at least by Millennials. There are three primary things they are looking for in a spiritual leader, and these three things, if not found, will absolutely keep them from engaging in church. First, they are looking for integrity. In the Sacred Roots study, 35 percent of Millennials said that their negative perception of church was a result of moral failures in church leadership.[28] Second, they want leadership to be authentic and relatable. They do not expect their leaders to be just like them, but they do expect their leader to be honest, communicate their own struggles as human beings, and to be themselves. Finally, Millennials want their leaders to be the people to provide vision and to facilitate participation and implementation of the vision. They key word here is *facilitate*. Millennials want to be part of something bigger than themselves, are highly collaborative, and ultimately, they want to have a voice. They want leaders who will share power, mentor them, and bring them along in the process.

BECOMING GUIDES NOT GURUS

Parents want their pastors to help guide them and not just tell them what to do. Your role, in the life of a young family, is that of a coach. You must come alongside them and help them process, help them do the work, and help them find the best ways to do it. Are you picking up on who does most of the work here? They do. You are an instigator, a navigator, a guide.

It's been said that the best way to determine if you are a leader is to look behind you. If no one is following you then you are just taking a walk.[29] Millennials don't want to just follow the leader, they want to be part of the leader's team. This is the most effective way to get buy-in from any group of people.[30] If you want to reach Millennials as parents then you must find a place for them to belong and contribute. They are not a passive audience; they are more educated and entrepreneurial than their parents or grandparents and want to help you build something great.

Guiding parents toward Jesus requires you to discover where they need Jesus the most. Each of us needs salvation: this is a good place to start. But each of us also needs Jesus in areas of finance, relationships, and discipline. Which of these needs best resonate with your young parents? Pick the best Jesus-destination and lead them there. It matters less where you are going and more that you go together. Remember to let your parents determine the route, the detours, and the pace.[31] Guides keep their patrons moving in the right direction but don't necessarily set the pace or agenda. This ownership is essential to the task.[32] It is essential to the success of discipleship in your own church. Perhaps Ross Parsley puts it best when he says, "creating opportunities for young and inexperienced leaders is one of the most effective tools we have to continue to make the church relevant and dynamic to our culture."[33]

DIGITAL NATIVES

The first generation to be born into digital technology, Millennials are also the most technologically connected generation. Technology has provided them with endless information and entertainment, as well as myriad sources for social connection and expression.[34] With this technological upbringing come strengths and weaknesses. Their technological adeptness allows them to offer a unique and necessary set of skills to other generations in the workforce.[35] They are more naturally innovative than previous generations, especially with the technological tools they have at their disposal. Over the past two decades, there has been a significant surge, and even redefining of entrepreneurship in America, and we have many Millennials to thank for this.[36] In the past, starting a business was a high-risk endeavor that required a significant investment of both time and money, as well as possible schooling. Today, a person can start a business using an app they've downloaded on their iPad or phone.

While the strengths of their technological adeptness result in productivity and innovation in the workplace, the weaknesses that have developed as a byproduct of technology are primarily relational in nature. Because of texting and social media, Millennials can lack the communication skills that are required to have difficult conversations or address conflict.[37] They can also lack emotional intelligence and are less empathetic than other generations because of their lack of person-to-person experience. Additionally, with the internet at their fingertips and the already established drive-through, make-it-my-way culture they've grown up in, they've been conditioned to expect instant results and often tend to have unrealistic expectations about change and career advancement.

USING DIGITAL TOOLS

Let us take some pressure off of you right now: You do not need to become a computer whiz. You do, however, need to recognize that communication has changed dramatically over the past few years. In order to be heard you must pick up a few new tricks. It's easy to dismiss a lot of the changes in communication as trendy; but remember that you are speaking to the first generation to grow up in a world where the Internet is always on, phones have touch screens, and tablets are have replaced babysitters. In short, you need to recognize that these digital tools were the first tools many Millennials learned how to use.[38] This digital revolution represents one of the greatest cultural shifts in generations. Future generations may consider the Internet, and its many access points, as being more influential than the radio, telegraph, and telephone combined.

The advance in technology today has made our tools more affordable and accessible than ever before.[39] They are constantly changing with life cycles measured in months instead of years.[40] More has changed in the past ten years than the past one hundred. So how is it possible for us to keep up? How can we find the time to communicate through a language that is constantly changing? The answer is this: You can't.

You must strike a balance between new and effective. When it comes to social networks, the second mouse always gets the cheese. It rarely pays to be on the cutting edge. The same is true for your adoption of new communication tools. For some of you this is a relief, for others this is a huge disappointment. We feel for you. The cutting edge is exciting, new, and full of potential; it seems to be where *real* innovators live and breathe and make an impact on the world. Actually, this is not usually how things work: real cutting-edge innovators are people you have never heard of. Apple is infamously one step behind the "competition." They are never the first to adopt new technology but they are often considered the best at refining someone else's big breakthrough. You must find a digital "sweet spot" and learn how to master a few tools instead of dabbling in many.

We are not going to list potential communication tools in this chapter. But we will say this: view each tool as a communication medium and not as a technological medium. When you realize the nature of these tools, be they email or social networks, you begin to see how information is delivered and received. Find someone to help you develop effective strategies for each tool. Resist moving on to the "next thing" until you have mastered and milked the tools that your current strategy is using. An excellent X-strategy always trumps a mediocre X-Y-Z strategy. How you choose to communicate with Millennials and their kids says a lot about you. Mediums communicate meaning.[41] Pick the best one for you and don't be afraid to ask another digital native to help you get your message across.

CONCLUSION

Millennials are parents now and your ministry must be prepared to reach out to them. They view the world through a very different lens and expect to follow a different type of pastor through a different type of world.

REFLECTION QUESTIONS

1. How can you create a culture of grace and truth in your church?
2. What can you do to lead more authentically?
3. Who can you collaborate with to develop technology strategies and tools?
   4. How can you foster conversation and community in your church?

END OF CHAPTER NOTES

[6] Pew Research Center, "Millennials in Adulthood," *Pew Research Center's Social & Demographic Trends Project*, http://www.pewsocialtrends.org/2014/03/07/millennials-in-adulthood/ (accessed September 29, 2015).

[7] Samantha Raphelson, "Amid The Stereotypes, Some Facts About Millennials," *NPR.org*, http://www.npr.org/2014/11/18/354196302/amid-the-stereotypes-some-facts-about-millennials (accessed September 29, 2015).

[8] Pew Research Center, "Millennials in Adulthood."

[9] Pew Research Center, "Millennials in Adulthood."

[10] Tom Rath and Barry Conchie, *Strengths Based Leadership: Great Leaders, Teams, and Why People Follow* (New York: Gallup Press, 2008).

[11] Patrick Lencioni, *Getting Naked: A Business Fable About Shedding the Three Fears That Sabotage Client Loyalty* (San Francisco: Jossey-Bass, 2010).

[12] Malcolm Gladwell, *David and Goliath: Underdogs, Misfits, and the Art of Battling Giants* (New York: Little, Brown and Company, 2013).

[13] Andy Stanley, *Next Generation Leader: 5 Essentials for Those Who Will Shape the Future* (Sisters, Ore.: Multnomah Books, 2006).

[14] Stephen R. Covey, *Principle-Centered Leadership* (New York: Fireside Press, 1992).

[15] Chantelle St. Clair, "Disengaging From Stereotypes: Evolution of Entrepreneurs," *LinkedIn Pulse*,

https://www.linkedin.com/pulse/disengaging-from-stereotypes-evolution-entrepreneurs-st-clair (accessed September 29, 2015,).

[16] Christian Smith et al., *Lost in Transition: The Dark Side of Emerging Adulthood*(New York: Oxford University Press, 2011), p. 36.

[17] Ephesians 2:8–9, NIV

[18] Gabe Lyons, *The Next Christians: The Good News About the End of Christian America* (New York: Doubleday Religion, 2010).

[19] 1 John 4:19, ESV.

[20] Tim Kimmel, *Connecting Church & Home* (Nashville: Randall House, 2013).

[21] Jon Tyson and Barna Group, *Sacred Roots: Why the Church Still Matters* (Grand Rapids, Mich.: Zondervan, 2014).

[22] Tyson and Barna Group.

[23] Tim Elmore and Dan Cathy, *Generation iY: Our Last Chance to Save Their Future* (Atlanta, Ga.: Poet Gardener Publishing, 2010).

[24] Louis A. Markos, "Belonging Before Believing," *ChristianityToday.com*, http://www.christianitytoday.com/ct/2007/february/43.124.html (accessed September 29, 2015).

[25] Howard Hendricks, *Teaching to Change Lives: Seven Proven Ways to Make Your Teaching Come Alive* (Sisters, Ore.: Multnomah Books, 2003).

[26] Brian Haynes, *Shift: What It Takes to Finally Reach Families Today* (Loveland, Colo.: Group Publishing, 2009).

[27] Roy H. Williams and Michael R. Drew, *Pendulum: How Past Generations Shape Our Present and Predict Our Future* (New York: Vanguard Press, 2012).

[28] George Barna, "What Millennials Want When They Visit Church," Barna Group, March 3, 2015, https://www.barna.org/barna-update/millennials/711-what-millennials-want-when-they-visit-church#.VTmBia1Viko.

[29] John C. Maxwell, *The 21 Irrefutable Laws of Leadership: Follow Them and People Will Follow You*, (Nashville: Thomas Nelson, 2007).

[30] Peter M. Senge, *The Fifth Discipline: The Art and Practice of the Learning Organization* (New York: Doubleday/Currency, 2006).

[31] George Barna, *Revolution* (Carol Stream, Ilinois: Tyndale Momentum, 2012).

[32] Martin Linsky and Ronald A. Heifetz, *Leadership on the Line: Staying Alive through the Dangers of Leading* (Boston, Mass.: Harvard Business Review Press, 2002).

[33] Ross Parsley, *Messy Church: A Multigenerational Mission for God's Family*, New edition (Colorado Springs: David C. Cook, 2012).

[34] Pew Research, "Millennials: A Portrait of Generation Next" (Pew Research Center, February 2010), p. 25, http://www.pewsocialtrends.org/files/2010/10/millennials-confident-connected-open-to-change.pdf.

[35] Pew Research, "Millennials."

[36] St. Clair, "Disengaging From Stereotypes."

[37] Elmore and Cathy, *Generation iY*.

[38] Brandon Vogt, *The Church and New Media: Blogging Converts, Online Activists, and Bishops Who Tweet* (Huntington, Ind: Our Sunday Visitor, 2011).

[39] Peter H. Diamandis and Steven Kotler, *Bold: How to Go Big, Create Wealth and Impact the World* (New York: Simon & Schuster, 2015).

[40] Andy Crouch, *Culture Making: Recovering Our Creative Calling* (Downers Grove, Ill: IVP Books, 2008).

[41] John Dyer and T. David Gordon, *From the Garden to the City: The Redeeming and Corrupting Power of Technology* (Grand Rapids, Mich.: Kregel Publications, 2011).

PART FIVE: SCIENCE

Science describes the critical insight gained from academic research about the world that God has made. By taking a closer look at the functions of the brain, psychosocial development, and learning styles you will become a better teacher and volunteer trainer. Our first idea will help you understand how kids grow up. It introduces ideas about developmental psychology and will help you understand what types of things kids are processing for each stage of life. The second chapter discusses how technology is impacting the brain, particularly the brains of children. This chapter ends with a few ideas to help you do a better job integrating technology into your own ministry. The third, and final, chapter discusses the learning styles of children. If you have never considered how children learn differently, then this chapter is for you.

5.1 UNDERSTANDING HOW KIDS GROW UP
Amy Johnson

As children's pastors and leaders, we are on a mission to fulfill a direct order from Jesus. As we pursue our portion of the Great Commission, I believe we can be more effective if we begin to look deeper into the psychology of how children learn and develop.

It is important to look at psychological theories from the past and research what key theorists such as Freud, Piaget, and Erikson have to say about what our children require at different stages of life. It is also good to do some personal studies into the ever-changing mind of a child. We need to learn the basic age-appropriate needs of the students in our care, and look deeper into their spiritual needs. It is important, when analyzing children's learning fundamentals, to acknowledge that our mission is to go beyond teaching the Bible for content, and instead expose children to how to apply that content to their lives, leading students into forever relationships with the Creator.

To understand how to reach students with the gospel of Jesus Christ, we must first understand the basic stages of their development.

These stages are as follows:

Stage 1: Infancy/Baby. The development happening in infancy is simply amazing. As soon as children are born, they almost instantly begin bonding with others. In the infancy stage, as long as basic needs are met, they will mature. Infants learn quickly how demand and response works: "When I cry, my mom or dad respond, they fulfill my needs and it's all good!"

Infancy is also the beginning of a child's journey toward developing self-esteem. The infant begins to grasp this concept: "I mean something to you, because when I cry you fix the problem." Love is shown thorough the receiving of a bottle, a snuggle, or a new diaper. The infant demands and the caretaker responds. The key therefore to a smooth-running church nursery in the eyes of the infant is that the baby's needs are met quickly, the baby is shown love, and the baby feels safe.

Stage 2: Toddler/ Preschooler. Some new and exciting things begin to happen for toddlers. As they become free to explore their surroundings, they begin to experience freedom and a new stage of development. What occurs during this stage is, "I can make my own choices." The toddler begins making limited choices and gets to decide, "Will I explore here or will I explore over there"? They make choices about what foods they like, when they will potty-train, and if and when they will clean up their toys. The key here is, *I get to choose!* With this beginning of choice, the two-year-old's favorite word may become "no."

Self-expression and emotional discovery is important in toddlerhood. Toddlers may discover that they like some people more than others. They may get angry when they don't get their own way or feel sad when they get in trouble; they are learning how to please people and how to upset them as well. Toddlers are growing at a rapid rate both physically and mentally. At this young age, preschoolers learn how to reason. They also learn that they can affect others. Toddlers are becoming proficient in basic skills and are expert explorers of their environment. Like sponges, their brains are soaking up everything they come into contact with.

Stage 3: School Age. School-age children (aged six to twelve) are on a journey of academic learning and are still learning at a rapid rate. They are learning a lot of factual knowledge, and are also beginning to ask questions about who they are and what they believe. Students are seeking approval. They are longing for a cheerleader and they want guidance. At the same time, they now need to find things out and do things on their own. Autonomy is quite important for the school-age child. Just to prove to themselves that they can, they will begin to try new and harder things.

Your average school-age child strongly desires to please his or her parents, teachers, and caregivers. However, school-age children are beginning to have their first taste of defeat and failure. They're experiencing their first misspelled words and their first lost homework assignments. The school-age child will also experience their first real consequences for making bad choices. When bad choices are made and consequences are doled out, school-age children desperately need to know that they are still loved and cared for. When given encouragement, support and positive feedback we see these students do great things!

Stage 4: Adolescents/Teenagers. Adolescence (ages thirteen to eighteen years) is one of the toughest stages of childhood. Bodies begin to change and hormones begin to take over. Not only do children change physically, but emotionally as well. It would be somewhat accurate to call these the "rollercoaster years." Teenagers are driven by a need for independence, and yet they have a longing to belong to a community and a strong desire to know that they are accepted as well as loved. The middle school and high school years are full of insecurity, peer pressure, and moodiness. However, from these years comes vast amounts of personal growth, social skill development, mastery of talents and gifting, and the ability to make lasting friendships. Talented teenagers are capable and make amazing leaders when given the best tools and the right amount of encouragement.

How do these developmental stages affect the spiritual formation needs of our students? How do we as pastors and children's leaders reach these kids? How do we meet them at the point where they will hear and receive what we have to say? And how do we go beyond teaching the Bible for only its content to also instilling in students the core values of walking in relationship with God? Let's look at some ways we can accomplish this.

Nursery. Having a clean, safe environment with kind and loving leaders is key. Parents need to know that their babies are safe and cared for.

Happy Parents + Happy Leaders = Happy Babies

Having Christian music or godly infant videos playing in the background can be great. The biggest key at this age level, however, is to have the babies in the hands of caregivers who love Jesus. You are looking for workers who have proven to show patience as well as godly character. When choosing nursery workers, be careful. Just because someone volunteers does not make the person qualified. The way someone speaks to children and to each other will set the mood. Little ones absorb everything.

Toddlers/Preschoolers. Toddlers are like little sponges. We need to provide an environment where they can learn. It is great if your Bible story includes objects because they can see and touch them. The more ways you can reinforce a simple concept, the better. Have several choices for the toddlers. They are learning to choose, and a busy toddler is a happy toddler. Have consistent, loving discipline. At this stage of development you want to reinforce the right things. Correction must come in a positive and consistent way. In Dr. Kevin Leman's book, *Making Children Mind Without Losing Yours,* he graphs what kids of this age and stage need in a responsible parent or (in our case) a good leader.[42]

Good leaders will:

- Give children choices and formulate guidelines for them.
- Provide children with opportunities to make decisions.
- Develop consistent, loving discipline.
- Hold children accountable.
- Let reality be the teacher.
- Convey respect, self-worth and love to the child, thereby enhancing the child's self-esteem.

Children at this age are deciding who they are and what they believe about themselves. Our job as leaders is to provide them with undeniable proof that they are loved by us and by God.

School Age. School-age children are so much fun. They are excited to learn, and more than anything they want acceptance and independence. Students of this age are ready to make some decisions about what and whom they believe in. Our job at this point is to show them what it means to have a relationship with Christ. As much as we want to teach them the contents of the Bible, it is equally important to teach them how the Bible relates to their lives. In my experience, students aged eight to twelve want to understand who Jesus is, what Jesus expects from them, and how they can accomplish doing what God wants. It is important to explain the concepts of grace and redemption. Remember school-age kids are in the stage where as much as they want to please, they are also making mounds of mistakes. Grade school is the introduction to peer pressure and fitting into to the right crowd. By providing them with the right tools, we teach them how to cope with temptation and overcome shortcomings. This will go a long way in leading them to a decision to say yes to Jesus.

Teenagers. Most of us doing kids' ministries are not directly overseeing youth. This does not, however, mean we should not strive to understand the heart and mind of the adolescent. Teens can be some of the absolute best children's ministries leaders. If they are students who have come through our ministry, they already understand how it all works. Youth want to belong to a community. Allow them to become a part of our teams and they will shine. Require a certain level of conduct from them and we will help them to stay accountable. Plug them into our programs once or twice a month and then encourage them to attend adult services as well. I have learned that the kids who have gotten involved in teaching and service to the kids over the years have been more likely to stay in church. Youth need to have a purpose, and I will be the one to give them one. Remember to be real with them, encourage them, and celebrate their wins because school is often beating them into the ground, discouraging them at every turn. If I can provide a positive place for them, they will be an excellent resource for me as a leader!

I love what Don Detrick has to say in his book, *Growing Disciples Organically:* "Organic spiritual formation: The natural growth that occurs when authentic faith in Jesus Christ is merged with intentional alignment to the principles of Scripture and empowered by the Holy Spirit while living and serving together."[43] When we take our students who have graduated from kids' church and give them purpose and ministry, I believe that is organic growth.

On a good week, we may get to hang out with any given student for three or four hours. Our students spend time under the influence of many other things and people for the remaining 100+ waking hours of their week. We need intentionally to make sure the little time we have with our students is effective. Our responsibility is hugely important. In Ted Tripp's book, *Shepherding a Childs Heart,* Tripp speaks from the perspective of a parent. He explains that children are going to do one of two things: They are either going to accept the teaching that they are given from those presenting God to them, or they are going to reject the teaching of God given to them and search for answers elsewhere.[44]

What are we doing as children's leaders to improve the chances that our students will accept the gospel message? I suggest we make sure we are doing our job with purpose and excellence. Perhaps the following guidelines will help us to be effective in our ministry as we set out to do God's work.

HAVE A CLEAR GOAL

What do you want your students to glean from you before they leave your ministry? Ten years ago I was deciding my ministry goal. I was fairly new to children's ministries and I had no idea what I was doing. A friend of mine in children's ministries asked me why I was a children's pastor. I had to think long and hard. It took me a while before I came up with the answer, but now I know without a shadow of a doubt that I am a children's pastor because I want families to go to heaven. I know that people who get saved as children are more likely to grow up to adults who serve Jesus. Kids need hope. What is your purpose and why do you do this? You need to know because purpose drives us to be effective.

BE PASSIONATE

Children are very perceptive and will see the excitement that flows through you. I have indeed had days where I did not want to be in church. On those days it is not uncommon to have a child ask me "Pastor Amy, is everything OK?" When we are passionate about what we believe the kids will be excited to hear that message. I love the quote by Benjamin Franklin, "Purpose is the reason you journey. Passion is the fire that lights your way." When we light a fire under ourselves, the love of Jesus will shine through us. Kids need Jesus!

BE AUTHENTIC

Have you ever sat in a service or had a conversation with someone and all you could think was, "Wow, they are fake!" Who wants to hang with a phony? Once again kids are perceptive. Try to enjoy what you do. When I am trying to fake it, kids will eventually see through me. What are you doing to insure that you are being real? Kids are generally easy to please, if you take the time to ask how they are and give them a word of encouragement, or a smile, they will love you. No need to try too hard to please. Just be real with them.

BUILD RELATIONSHIPS

Investing in the lives of your students is a vital part of taking your ministry to the next level. Students will come and go in our lives. We feel stronger connections to some kids than others. I believe that the Holy Spirit brings kids into my ministry life, and that I need to respond. There are times when I have felt hurt when a student leaves my ministry. There have been times when students I have invested in have turned away from God. There have even been times when students have gone to be with Jesus way too early and that hurts deeply. But, there have also been times when students have come to me crying, all grown up and ready to return to Jesus. Having a student in your office reminds you that you invested in him or her. Having them rededicate their hearts to Jesus as they kneel on the floor of your office makes it all worth the investment. It will be worth it!

Mark Batterson, an amazing man of faith, sums up why we work so hard to understand the little hearts of the kids we work with: "I have an unshakable sense of destiny because I know that as long as I pursue God's calling on my life, then God is ultimately responsible for getting me where He wants me to go."[45] We have to trust that God is going to lead us into understanding what our kids need both spiritually and emotionally. So here we go—we are in this together. Let's get out there and spread some love as Jesus changes some lives!

REFLECTION QUESTIONS

1. How will you help your teachers become more aware of the developmental stages of children?
2. What are the clear goals of your ministry?
3. How do you know if you are being authentic with the people in your church?

END OF CHAPTER NOTES

[42] Dr. Kevin Leman, *Making Children Mind without Losing Yours* (Grand Rapids, Mich.: Revell, 2005).

[43] Don Detrick, *Growing Disciples Organically: The Jesus Method of Spiritual Formation* (Sisters, Ore.: Deep River Books, 2013), p. 250.

[44] Tedd Tripp, *Shepherding a Child's Heart* (Wapwallopen, Penn.: Shepherd Press, 1995).

[45] Mark Batterson, *In a Pit with a Lion on a Snowy Day: How to Survive and Thrive When Opportunity Roars* (Sisters, Ore.: Multnomah Books, 2006).

5.2 HOW TECHNOLOGY IMPACTS A CHILD'S BRAIN
Brent Colby

Our world has been revolutionized by smaller, faster, and cheaper computers that fit into our pockets. We are living in an age where the world's information is only a tap away. Warehouses of computers work to digitize the sum of human knowledge every second of the day. In 2014, Facebook users shared 2.5 million pieces of content, Twitter users tweeted 300,000 times, and YouTubers uploaded seventy-two hours of video . . . every minute of the day.[46] Language, art, history, and science are rendered to bits and bytes that can be recalled instantly. A new generation of people are solving world problems from the comfort of their homes; leveraging international resources from the same stream that delivers television and games. Barriers are being torn down which once made learning, communication, and commerce impossible. Technology has empowered billions to understand, connect, and care. But vertigo is beginning to plague our ascent toward this digital altruism.

Technology has begun to cripple our capacity to think, create, and have meaningful relationships with each other. We have traded independence for convenience, entertainment for creativity, and access for empathy. Scientific studies are beginning to reveal the profound impact that technology is having on the brain. But the purchases of progress have cost us; the technological revolution is not without causalities.

Children are growing up in the most technologically advanced society that the world has ever known. Technology is having a significant impact on the adolescent brain. This generation of children is the first to grow up with connected devices near their cribs, couches, and cars. As a result, they are being taught to think differently than any other generation before them. Children's pastors must be aware of these influences and teach kids in ways that leverage the best that technology has to offer while avoiding its negative effects.

We must be careful not to paint technology as a villain or hero in these pages because it is inanimate and amoral. Technology, in itself, has no ethical bearings; we are the ones who give it meaning. It is as good as we are good, and bad as we are bad. However, we must also acknowledge that technology is powerful. With it we magnify the best and worst that our world has to offer. Perhaps Melvin Kranzberg says it best: "technology is neither good nor bad, neither is it neutral." [47] We respect technology for the great influence it has over society today. It opens doors to great possibilities and amplifies the desires, goals, and ambitions of our culture.

I am using a single word to describe a coalition of devices, services, and access points that shape our lives. Think of computing devices such as laptops, phones, televisions, gaming consoles, tablets, and wearables when you read the word "technology." But also think of the programs that run on these devices that enable us to play games, watch videos, listen to music, rent cars, book hotels, order groceries, and build relationships. I am painting with broad strokes because I am trying to prove a broad point: Technology is impacting the way kids think, therefore we should reconsider how we use technology in our ministry. We will start with a quick description of how the brain works, describe how this function is impacted by technology, and establish guidelines for the use of technology in your church today.

How the Brain Works

Behind your eyes and between your ears lies the most wonderful part of God's creation. Your brain is as heavy as a cantaloupe and as complex as the universe. It receives everything you sense, controls everything you do, and is the clearinghouse for your every emotion. It has stumped scientists for generations; only recently have we been allowed to peek behind the curtain and understand the wonder of the human brain.

If you look at a human brain you will notice it looks gross. OK, perhaps that is a personal reaction but no, seriously, it is all wrinkly and slimy. The wrinkles are important, they are called *sulci* and *gyri* and they afford the brain more surface area. Surface area is where much of the cerebral processing takes place. Scientists say the brain slime, or cerebral spinal fluid, is there to protect the brain. (I think that the slime is there so we don't touch it, which I guess is another way of protecting the brain.) It can be divided into a few parts whose names you might recognize, including the frontal lobes, hypothalamus, and medulla oblongata. Most parts of the brain have a specific job to do. For example: the frontal lobes deal with sound, music, face, and object recognition while the occipital lobes focus on visual processing.[48] Each of these regions perform a specific function while retaining a high level of adaptability. "Plasticity" is the term used to describe the brain's ability to change and adapt.[49] Each of these regions is constantly responding to external forces. It is a beautiful part of God's design, which we are still trying to fully understand

The wonder of the brain comes into focus when we take a closer look. Your brain is made of two types of cells. These are called nerve cells and glial cells.[50] The latter hold the brain together while maintaining a healthy environment for the former. The nerve cells, or neurons, are where the action happens and come in a variety of shapes and sizes. The basic anatomy of a neuron consists of a core (nucleus) with an extension of arms (dendrite, axon, and synapse). Each of these arms is part of a system designed to send and receive messages from other nuclei. These messages are encoded through a complex series of chemical and electrical reactions. Chemicals such as noradrenaline, serotonin, and dopamine are the major players here. The neurons are networked together throughout the nervous system and pass along every type of information at lightning speed. Every movement, sensation, and memory is run through this system of neurons. It works faster than you can consciously think and manages the most complex system that the world has ever known.

The power of the brain is found in the connection between neurons. A neuron, by itself, does not have the capacity to move a finger. But a *team* of neurons can build cathedrals, compose symphonies, or invent Hot Pockets. Recent developments in the laboratory have allowed us to observe these connections in action.[51] Today we can see how the sound of a bell, touch of a hand, or smell of food triggers automatic responses in the brain. Neurons exchange electrical pulses between millions of synapses and initiate voluntary and involuntary responses throughout the body. The establishment of these pathways has a strong influence on how we respond to the world around us. You have conditioned yourself to do X when Y happens. The challenge today is that we experience many more X's than our grandparents, parents, or older siblings ever did.

The brain processes information in a remarkable way. It actively prioritizes whatever we think, sense, and feel. That is right; your brain *does* have a filter and it uses it all of the time. Consider this: Your body is constantly bombarded with stimuli including sights, sounds, and smells. Your brain is taking in all of this information while making adjustments to your heart rate, body temperature, or digestion. Meanwhile, it is enabling conscious movements such as walking, talking, or reading. Not to mention that your brain is also finding ways to capture, store, and recall everything you have ever experienced! It is impossible for you to consciously process even a small part of this information. In fact, many scholars believe that we can only process one voluntary thing at a time.[52] Multitasking is a myth and your brain knows it. Your brain filters out the things that require your attention from the things that can run automatically. Scholars refer to this action as an "opportunity of cost."[53] You might call it subconscious decision-making.

Your brain hasn't always been so smart. You and the world around you have been teaching it from the very beginning. You develop a sense of taste, smell, and sound in utero.[54] It is possible for a child's brain to begin development before a mother knows she is pregnant.[55] This means that a child's brain is developing connections between synapses very early on; they are learning from the very beginning. Studies have even observed newborns crying with French or German accents depending on their mother's native language.[56] The connections we make establish powerful patterns that influence our ability to learn, make decisions, and build relationships with others.

How Technology Affects the Brain

Technology changes our relationship with ideas and information. It also changes how we relate to each other and the world. Today we have more interactions than any previous generation, however, each of these interactions contain less meaning than ever before. Our cell phones and computers automate countless routine tasks, even those with real people. This automation, "alters the character of the entire task, including the roles, attitudes, and skills of the people who take part in it."[57] And so it becomes easier for us to be less connected to the things and the people around us.

Every time you touch a phone, computer, or remote control, something powerful is happening in your brain. Your brain anticipates these connections and becomes habituated to them, creating physical, mental, and emotional patterns. In one famous example from 2009, a teenage girl sent more than 14,000 texts in a single month.[58] That is more than one text for every two minutes of the day. You may not consider yourself *addicted* to your phone; but you should realize that you are creating bonds between it and your brain.[59] You may not have an addictive personality, but each of us is a potential addict.

Our constant interaction with technology causes anxiety and robs us of quiet times. When was the last time you were bored? Many children will never know what it is to be bored in a car, at a restaurant, or at home. Every moment of the day can be spent in the company of a game, video, or social network. Scholars remind us that, "It's not only deep thinking that requires a calm, attentive mind. It's also empathy and compassion."[60] Children who are growing up distracted may never develop a mature sense of empathy.

Overdependence on technology also hinders our ability to think critically. We live among computers whose goal is to produce a constant flow of relevant content. Our maps, searches, and emails are embedded with information and advertisements selling us on what we need to know. Children today expect online searches, apps, and devices to know what they need to know. They are learning to depend on technology to determine what is most important. We often allow ourselves to exchange knowledge for information. Carr believes that, "the strip-mining of relevant content replaces the slow excavation of meaning."[61]

TECHNOLOGY IN CHILDREN'S MINISTRY

We must be aware of the influence that technology has over this emerging generation. Scholars are correct when they say that, "we become, neurologically, what we think."[62] *How* we think determines *what* we think. Thinking like a robot generates robotic ideas while thinking like a human generates humane thoughts, feelings, and concepts. The discipleship of children in our ministries cannot be automated. It is something that may be inspired by the church but is executed by the family. It happens at home, on the road, and before we go to bed.[63] We need to develop spiritually mature children—and there will never be an app for that.

How can we create powerful learning environments that emphasize relationships, transformation, and retention? My goal is not to dissuade you from the use of technology in your ministry today. However, let me suggest three strategies that will help you speak to the heart of this plugged-in generation. It starts by developing a ministry that is based on relationship. It continues by creating an environment of creativity instead of consumption, and ends with you being awesome.

Build relationships with children. You and your volunteers are the most influential resource that your church will ever have. Videos, lights, or games will never become more important than the personal interactions that you will have with children. Videos, games, and lights are not bad, but they must not become the focal point of your ministry. Create space for personal interaction to take place. We can fall into the trap of letting the teaching material do the talking for us. No kid has ever had his or her life changed by curriculum. *People* change people, and this transformation doesn't happen by mistake.

Andrew Newberg and Mark Waldman describe how complex human-to-human interaction really is. They say that, "human communication is one of the most complex neural processes in the brain. It involves face and voice recognition, language processing, memory recall, speech coordination, concept recognition, imagery mapping, emotional regulation, deceit and fairness evaluation, strategic planning, and the activation of neural circuits governing volitional activities and behavior."[64] Have you created an environment where kids have room to do all this processing? Sure, most of it happens in the background processes of our brain, but a lot of it requires actual focus. Do you put as much effort toward crazy as you do contemplation? Make space for meaningful conversations. Remember that each phase of growth is accompanied by significant relationships.[65] Find ways to allow kids to talk, to process, and to think. Take away the distractions from your ministry and let the relational part of your ministry shine.

Kids learn by doing. Find ways to let your kids process the meaning of your ministry in a variety of ways. We are all familiar with learning styles[66] or multiple intelligences.[67] Remember that kids need to interact with ideas. Find ways to help them put their newfound insights into action. This can be through games, crafts, or activities. Give them something to hang the idea on and increase the likelihood of them taking it home. So often, we practice consumption Christianity—we "win" by digesting the most information. People have limits on how much information they can process. Andy Stanley encourages pastors to preach one big idea a week and to throw away the multi-point sermon.[68]

How then should we teach to kids? Reggie Joiner and his team from Think Orange have developed a simple model of teaching in which wonder, discovery, and passion are emphasized through the spiritual development of a child.[69] Jerome Berryman developed an entire model of ministry based on kids playing with ideas and objects surrounding God and his creation.[70] Do whatever you can to help kids engage with your message. Be creative, be fun, do something memorable.

My third and final idea for you is this: be awesome. It requires a bit of awe to inspire kids who are constantly bombarded with the distractions of technology today. You must find ways to blow their minds. In some ways, this is becoming easier than ever. As kids become more disconnected with the physical world, kinetic activities are reemerging as novelties. Throwing a ball, running a race, or preparing a snack may be more memorable today than ever before. How many kids in your ministry have pounded a nail, exploded a water bottle, or built a human pyramid? These activities ask children to participate in ways that are not demanded of them today.

You need to tap your inner awesomeness to bring about the wonder of Christ. How can you make your children's ministry a creative space where children go home having experienced something new? Each week you have the opportunity to push back on technological apathy. Use the gifts that God has given to you paint a fuller picture of who God is.

FINAL THOUGHT

Technology is changing the way kids experience life. We must reconsider how we tell them about Jesus and of his love for us. This chapter has provided a quick look at how the brain works and how it is being influenced by technology today. We understand that kids are particularly susceptible to technology's influence and how we can navigate these effects through meaningful planning.

Consider a few simple guidelines for the use of technology in your church today. Minister through relationships, encourage interaction, and communicate through the wonder of God. Do this and you can bridge the gap that stands between this generation and eternity.

REFLECTION QUESTIONS

1. How do you foster relationships between kids, leaders, and parents in your ministry?
2. How can you teach and engage other learning styles in your ministry?
3. How can you create a "wow" moment every weekend in your ministry?

END OF CHAPTER NOTES

[46] Susan Gunelius, "The Data Explosion in 2014. Minute by Minute—Infographic," *ACI*, http://aci.info/2014/07/12/ther datar explosionr inr 2014r minuter byr minuter infographic/ (accessed September 21, 2015).

[47] Kentaro Toyama, *Geek Heresy: Rescuing Social Change from the Cult of Technology* (New York: PublicAffairs, 2015).

[48] David A. Sousa, *How the Brain Learns* (Thousand Oaks, Calif: Corwin, 2011).

[49] Norman Doidge, *The Brain That Changes Itself: Stories of Personal Triumph from the Frontiers of Brain Science* (New York: Viking, 2007).

[50] Sousa, p. 602.

[51] Sousa, p. 602.

[52] Gary Keller and Jay Papasan, *The ONE Thing: The Surprisingly Simple Truth Behind Extraordinary Results* (Austin, Tex.: Bard Press, 2013).

[53] Asghar Iran-Nejad and Sally Ann Zengaro, "Opportunity Prioritization, Biofunctional Simultaneity, and Psychological Mutual Exclusion," *Behavioral and Brain Sciences* 36, no. 6 (December 2013): 696–97; discussion 707–26, doi:http://dx.doi.org.seu.idm.oclc.org/10.1017/S0140525X13001088.

[54] Anna Blasi, et al., "Early Specialization for Voice and Emotion Processing in the Infant Brain," *Current Biology* 21, no. 14 (July 2011): 1220–24, doi:10.1016/j.cub.2011.06.009.

[55] "Fetal Development: 1st Trimester," http://www.mayoclinic.org/healthy-lifestyle/pregnancy-week-by-

week/in-depth/prenatal-care/art-20045302 (accessed September 15, 2015).

[56] Birgit Mampe, et al., "Newborns' Cry Melody Is Shaped by Their Native Language," *Current Biology* 19, no. 23 (December 2009): 1994–97, doi:10.1016/j.cub.2009.09.064.

[57] Nicholas Carr and Jeff Cummings, *The Glass Cage: Automation and Us* (Brilliance Audio, 2014), p. 67.

[58] Susannah Cahalan, "This Kid's a Text Maniac," *New York Post*, January 11, 2009, http://nypost.com/2009/01/11/this-kids-a-text-maniac/.

[59] Nicholas Carr, *The Shallows: What the Internet Is Doing to Our Brains* (New York: W.W. Norton & Company, 2011).

[60] Carr, p. 220.

[61] Carr, p. 166.

[62] Carr, p. 33.

[63] Deuteronomy 6:7

[64] Andrew Newberg and Mark Robert Waldman, *How God Changes Your Brain: Breakthrough Findings from a Leading Neuroscientist* (New York: Ballantine Books, 2009), p. 222.

[65] Reggie Joiner and Kristen Ivy, *It's Just a Phase—So Don't Miss It: Why Every Life Stage of a Kid Matters and at Least 13 Things Your Church Should Do About It* (Cumming, Ga.: Orange, a division of The reThink Group, 2015).

[66] Cynthia Ulrich Tobias, *The Way They Learn* (Carol Stream, Ill.: Focus on the Family, 1998).

[67] Howard E. Gardner, *Multiple Intelligences: New Horizons in Theory and Practice* (New York: Basic Books, 2006).

[68] Andy Stanley and Lane Jones, *Communicating for a Change: Seven Keys to Irresistible Communication* (Sisters, Ore.: Multnomah Books, 2006).

[69] Joiner, *Think Orange*.

[70] Jerome Berryman, *Godly Play* (Minneapolis: Augsburg Books, 1995).

5.3 DISCOVERING THE LEARNING STYLES OF CHILDREN
Chantel Rohr

Fall's brilliant colors, delicious foods, and amazing smells always make me reminisce about past experiences One of my favorite fall memories is getting bundled up to explore a corn maze with friends. As we entered the maze, some friends would run ahead giggling as they poked their heads through the cornstalks. Then there were those friends who would holler back "What way do we go?" Finally there was always that one friend who had the map in hand keeping the rest of us on track so we wouldn't get lost. I was the one who liked to explore the maze but still had a map I could refer to if needed.

Many of my preferences and problem-solving techniques were influenced by the way I learn and process information best. That was the same for my friends, which is why we used different strategies. Just like the choices in the maze, our learning styles can affect the way each of us make decisions, come to an understanding, or even pick correct tools (such as maps or verbal cues) to help us create the best experience possible.

As a student, I was the one who could never sit still; I was always bouncing my legs or fiddling with whatever I could get my hands on. As soon as I stopped moving, I would become distracted. Even though some subjects were difficult for me, I fell in love with teaching. I dreamed of teaching kindergarten through second grade and integrating music and movement into the classroom. After graduating from high school, I went to Northwest University in Kirkland Washington and earned a BA in elementary education. During college I had the opportunity to learn about and practice implementing learning styles into classroom settings, which changed how I viewed teaching forever! It also made me aware of why I struggled to engage in a classroom setting. Throughout this chapter you will discover what learning styles are, how to identify these styles in children, and how to use that knowledge to engage kids to learn about Christ.

According to Neil Fleming's VAK model, there are three styles of learning: visual, auditory, and kinesthetic. A learning style is simply the way a person perceives and processes information or experiences. "Most people possess a dominant or preferred learning style; however some people have a mixed and evenly balanced blend of the three styles."[71]

Imagine it's Sunday, and you are teaching the story of Noah and the flood. You gather your props and illustrations to help the children engage, and the kids bring their favorite stuffed animal for the lesson. As you begin the lesson you describe how God asks Noah to build a boat. You invite Chris to demonstrate building the ark. You hand him a mallet and the golf tee and tell him to hammer it into the foam. He gives you the deer in headlights look so you demonstrate it for him and then he copies you. The storm is quickly approaching so the children pretend to load the ark with their stuffed animals. As you are going through the lesson you notice that Joey is having a hard time focusing while you teach; he seems to be distracted by his stuffed giraffe. To redirect his attention you ask him a question, and he is able to answer you perfectly. A little confused, you move on to the storm part of the lesson. You invite Ashley to create a storm by using the spray bottles (rain), fans (wind), and pots and pans (thunder). Of course she was so excited that she can't stop moving beforehand. You finally give her permission to make the storm. During the storm you realize Chris isn't engaging in the story. As the storm stops, you put up an image of a rainbow and notice you have finally caught his attention again. You think, "Phew, I didn't lose him." After the lesson you walk away thinking, "That didn't go quite as planned." You assume that many kids missed parts of the story, but much o your surprise, the kids retell the whole story perfectly. You ask yourself, "How did that happen?" This is the beauty of engaging every learning style. Let's break it down further:

Visual learners. In the example above, Chris is your strong visual learner. He processes information best by being able to *see* what he is learning, which is why he did better with the demonstration and images than with verbal cues and noises. Visual learners enjoy pictures or books that have lots of imagery so they can vividly picture it in their minds. You'll often catch them doodling while they learn. When talking with them, they may use language such as, I can't *imagine*. . . . I *see*. . . . Can you *show* me?

Auditory learners. Joey represents your auditory learner who processes information best by listening and talking. Auditory learners have very strong listening skills and don't need to have eye contact to understand what you are saying, which is why Joey answered your question so easily. These learners often like to repeat instructions out loud or talk to themselves while they are discovering something new. Unlike Chris, these learners prefer you to *tell* them instructions rather than read instructions or follow a demonstration. Auditory learners say phrases such as, I didn't *hear.* . . . It *sounds* like. . . . Can you *tell* me?

Kinesthetic learners. Kinesthetic learners like Ashley process information best by using movement or a hands-on approach. They want to be able to touch, feel, and experiment with whatever they are learning about. You can spot them from a distance because they tend to talk with their hands. In conversations they will say things like: Can I *touch.* . . . I don't *feel* like. . . . I want to *move.* . . . Can I *try*?

Rita Dunn, director over studies on learning styles at St. John University, researched how implementing the Fleming's VAK model improves test scores. In this study, she found that two schools that accommodated learning styles into their curriculum were able to increase their test scores by 53 percent within three years.[72] I don't know about you, but I don't just want to reach a small percent of the kids for Christ. I want to reach 100 percent of them!

Let's think back to the Noah's ark scenario. How did visual, auditory, and kinesthetic learners engage in the story? For the visual learners, our use of stuffed animals, images, and visual props provided opportunities for them to use their dominant learning style. They could also engage through reading Scriptures, using picture books, or creating a rain chart. Auditory learners processed information by listening to the story, as well as hearing the thunder created by the pots and pans. Children who learn audibly also love opportunities to ask or answer questions, sing or play instruments, or have the chance to role-play for the lesson. Last but not least, the kinesthetic learners experienced the story with their hands as they used props (stuffed animals, storm props) recreating the story. These types of learners also enjoy doing actions such as swaying back and forth simulating the storm, or using clay to create a boat.

Using your knowledge of learning styles, how can you engage visual, auditory, and kinesthetic learners with the lessons you and your team are teaching? As you prepare your lessons, be aware of what your own dominant learning style is and which styles you struggle with. Most of us teach to our strength, but remember, not everyone processes information as you do. If your goal is to engage more children, you need to get out of your comfort zone. Have you ever experienced a time when you tried to explain or show someone how to do something, and they gave you a confused look? I sure have, and I've thought, "This is not that difficult to understand." This reminds me of a time in college when my now-husband and I went ice-skating. It was his first time, so he kept asking me "how's it work?" Of course as a kinesthetic learner I thought, "What do you mean how does it work? You put your skates on, get on the ice, and just start skating." I kept telling him, "You are overthinking this." Luckily he still chose to marry me! We quickly discovered that we are very different from each other. Because we process information differently we had to learn how to communicate with each other. We need to do the same for the kids in our ministry. If we want to engage more kids in learning about Christ, we need to meet the kids where they are just as Jesus does for us every day.

It is also important to note that each learning style has weaknesses. For example, visual learners' eyes catch everything. This makes them more susceptible to being distracted by kinesthetic learners who can't sit still. They can also be overwhelmed if there is too much visually going on in the room. Even though they like pictures and colors, they don't know where to focus their attention if there is too much to take in. Unlike visual learners, auditory learners are more oblivious to the items on the walls. They get distracted or over-stimulated with excess or unnecessary noise. Kinesthetic learners are famous for distracting or annoying these children with their pen-pushing or foot-tapping. Auditory learners are just as good at distracting others. These are the kids who walk into a quiet room and start talking to their friends rather than following the instructions written on the board. Kinesthetic learners can be easily distracted or disengaged when they are unable to move. These children can be "misdiagnosed as having ADHD or [being] troublemakers."[73] Being aware of these weaknesses will help you plan better so you know how to respond if a child is disengaging or causing distractions.

It's not your job to use all three learning styles simultaneously 100 percent of the time. That's impossible and will actually over-stimulate your learners. It is, however, your responsibility to be purposefully planning how to engage each learning style at some point in the time that you have with the kids. Using your knowledge of visual, auditory, and kinesthetic learners will help more children engage and experience Christ each week. And there is nothing better than watching kids as they discover who Jesus is and how they can be a part of his story.

Whether you are a pastor, volunteer, or parent, your knowledge of learning styles can drastically change your life and the lives of the children you are impacting for Christ each day!

Understanding how you personally process and learn will help you discover the learning styles of the kids in your ministry. Once you've done that you will know how to better communicate and engage those who differ from you. As you prepare to teach, use those learning styles to your advantage to engage kids. Think outside *your* box and reach more kids for Christ.

REFLECTION QUESTIONS

1. What differentiates each learning style?
2. What is your learning style?
3. Which learning style do you need to be more conscious about when teaching or communicating with others?
4. What are ways you can implement each learning style in your ministry area?

END OF CHAPTER NOTES

[71] "Visual, Auditory and Kinesthetic (VAK) Learning Style Model,"
http://www.jcu.edu.au/wiledpack/modules/fsl/JCU_090460.html (accessed October 2, 2015).

[72] Tina Barseghian and Jessica Kelmon, "Secrets to Raising Smart Kids: Determine Learning Style," *BabyCenter*, http://www.babycenter.com/0_secrets-to-raising-smart-kids-determine-learning-style_10336240.bc (accessed October 2, 2015).

[73] Fiona Baker, "Learning Styles in Children," *Kidspot.com*, http://www.kidspot.com.au/school/primary/learning-and-behaviour/learning-styles-in-children (accessed October 2, 2015).

PART SIX: STRATEGY

Strategy describes key organizational principles of children's ministry. No children's pastor has to be an expert in the field of team development, organizational systems, or communication, but they should be able to work competently in these areas. In this section we will take a quick look at three types of children's ministry strategy: the development of student leaders, special event scheduling, and communication. Student leaders are a key part of any successful children's ministry team. But few of us have experience working with students or student ministry. This first chapter will help you develop a plan to integrate high schoolers into your ministry. Designing an effective events calendar may be one of the most challenging, and effective ways to organize your ministry. This chapter is gold. Read it once then read it again. Finally we will discuss some basics of ministry communication. It's difficult to be heard in a world with more and more "noise." Discover some practical ways to connect with your families with more clarity, more often.

6.1 DEVELOPING STUDENT LEADERS
Jessica Downs

How did you get to where you are today? If you are reading this book, you are a likely a children's pastor or children's ministry leader. I want you to think for a moment . . . How old were you when you felt this calling on your life? Perhaps you stumbled into this position as an adult and really didn't see it coming. But if you're like me, you felt the Lord tugging on your heart at a pretty early age. I was about ten years old when God gave me a glimpse of what my future held and gave me a passion to teach little ones.

I always say that I served in the nursery as soon as I was out of the nursery, which may be a bit of an exaggeration, but not by much. I was given the tools and the opportunity to serve in various areas of children's ministry at my church when I was growing up. Now that could have been because our church didn't have a children's pastor the majority of my childhood, so they were always looking for volunteers. Or it could have been because I was the pastor's kid and I attended four services every Sunday. I mean, what else was I going to do?

Whatever the reason, I was given a chance to lead and because of that, my passion grew. I didn't do things perfectly. I'm sure I mixed up Jonah and Noah (I mean, really, their names sound a lot alike and both stories include boats!). I doubt I accurately explained the complexities of the Trinity and sanctification. My crafts? Nothing more than coloring pages and Play-Doh. But I was serving. And as I taught—if you can even call it that—God planted in my heart a desire for kids to know him. I wouldn't be where I am today if I hadn't been given a chance to learn and develop ministry skills in my teen years. How different would our lives look if we were never given a stage to practice on? Why is it, then, that we are so hesitant to allow young leaders a chance to grow in their skills on *our* stage?

Empowering, equipping and encouraging our young volunteers is an important key to health, both in their lives as well as our children's departments. Our role as children's pastor doesn't stop the third Sunday of June when our fifth-graders graduate into youth group. We still have a part to play in their development as leaders and as followers of Christ. If we are not making a conscious effort to empower, equip and encourage the young volunteers in our ministry, we are not doing our job.

EMPOWER

Student leaders will bring a whole different level to your children's ministry. They can relate to kids in a way we can't—it wasn't that long ago that they were sitting in those seats. They remember what caught their attention and what was boring. They are the ones who can tell us what we should change. And you know what? We need to hear them out. Their opinions are valuable and we should make sure they know that. Invite them to share ideas and concerns. If they are hesitant, provide a way for them to do it anonymously. Will they come up with crazy and unrealistic ideas? Probably, but I can pretty much guarantee you that their creativity will generate concepts you never would have thought of. Just a reminder: that's a good thing.

Beyond creating an environment in which student leaders know they can share their ideas, we should constantly look for ways to encourage their God-given talents. If you see something in one of your team members, don't be afraid to point it out and support them in it. You never know—you may be the one God uses to ignite a passion in them. You may be the only one speaking life and hope into the future of many young leaders.

Once we have determined strengths within our team, we need to offer students the freedom to stretch and grow, the freedom to fail and learn from it. As a leader, it can be difficult to give up the reins when you don't know how it will turn out. But how will your team get better if you don't give them the chance to try?

I sincerely hope you had the same liberty as you started out in your ministry. If you did, you know its benefits firsthand. If you didn't, I'd like you to take a moment and think about what it would have meant to have someone believe in you enough to include you in their ministry. Go ahead . . . think about it. Now, here's my challenge. Determine which aspects of the service you'd be willing to "give up" to allow your student leaders to grow. That may include skits, worship, offering, announcements, or even a lesson here and there.

Empowering our student leaders means more than just saying, "You can do this"; it requires letting them do it. Just like a plant that flourishes if given the proper nutrients and space, our student leaders have all the potential in the world. They simply need the right environment in order to release it.

Ready for a painfully obvious statement that we all too often forget? If we are not giving them room to grow, we are stifling them.

EQUIP

Now that we have empowered our young leaders, we need to take a serious look at how we can help them succeed. No one wants to be thrown into the ocean without first being taught how to swim. In the same way, we shouldn't toss our team members into a leadership position without first teaching them how to lead.

In order to effectively equip our student leaders we need to do three main things:

Communicate your expectations. Have them written out in a clear and concise manner—headlines and bullet points work well. Very few people will take an hour to go over a fifty-page volunteer handbook (let's just be honest—when was the last time you did?) If we expect certain behaviors we need to communicate those guidelines clearly. We can't expect what we don't express.

Give them what they need to do a good job. If we want excellence, we can't tell them what their role is right before a service. We must prepare beforehand so they can, too. If they are teaching, give them the lesson a couple of weeks in advance and check in with them to see if they need assistance. Do a run-through of the lesson with them and give pointers on how to make it even better. If they are planning the game, share some websites or resources that might be useful.

Train them. Whether you have an annual, semiannual, quarterly, or monthly training, *do it*. Put it on the schedule early and make sure your team knows about it well in advance. Follow up with lots of reminders—especially for your student leaders. Make your training sessions less than an hour and a half long, and always provide food!

My church is moving from a yearly training event to monthly ones. It's a big change and it will take a lot of time, energy, and resources, but I firmly believe these events will help our team be more effective and efficient. I adopted the idea after talking with a children's pastor in Florida, Aaron Strawn. He noticed that having monthly trainings gave him the opportunity to not only get more information across to his team, but the sessions brought unity and a buy-in that wasn't there before. He spends a good portion of their time together building up the team and having fun, then discusses the topic for the night and follows it up with food. His first month, thirty people attended. The next month there were sixty-five.

How much more effective would our trainings be if we were able to really spend time focusing on one or two topics at a time? Instead, if you're like me, we've been trying to jam-pack everything our team needs to know into one or two meetings, hoping they will attend and expecting them to catch and implement it all. Will all of our people make it each month? Probably not, but having lots of training opportunities at least increases the likelihood they'll make it to some!

Equipping our team takes time and effort, but it is vital to the health of our ministry and those who work beside us. Think of a football team with no pads or helmets; without the proper equipment, we can't expect them to win.

ENCOURAGE

This one comes naturally to some and not to others, but it is a very important piece of the puzzle. Have you ever met someone who doesn't like to be encouraged? It's possible you've come across someone who feels embarrassed because of the attention, but I guarantee that deep down, the recognition meant a lot to him or her.

The desire for affirmation is human nature. We shouldn't look to please man before God, but getting a pat on the back or a "way to go" helps keep all of us going. Our teens need it just as much as we do, if not more. They are in the stage of life where they are trying to figure out who they are now and who they want to be. We have the privilege of coming alongside and speaking positive words over them amidst the chaos and confusion.

One of the most important aspects of encouragement is building relationships with our teams. If we don't invest in them, they aren't going to invest in the ministry. So attend their events, send them an encouraging text, and let them know you are praying for them. But don't stop there: learn their birthdays, find out what someone's favorite candy is, or write cards and send them in the mail. On social media, praise their hard work and tag them and their parents. Go out of your way to applaud them in public and one-on-one. You may even consider planning an event for your youth leaders like bowling or game nights.

Let's be real . . . we all have days when we're not on our "A" game and need a little grace. We need to offer the same grace to our volunteers. They didn't go to school for this and frankly, they don't have to serve. People need to hear they are doing a good job, even if both of you know it could have gone more smoothly. Should we challenge them to be better? Absolutely! That is a huge part of their growth. But there is a right way and a wrong way to bring correction. Have you heard of the sandwich method? The idea is to:

1. determine what is going well,
2. share thoughts on how to improve, and
3. finish it off by either reiterating the positive or letting them know what could happen if your advice is followed.[74]

For example: "Chris, you are doing such a great job getting to know the kids in your small group. They really look up to you! To help get more conversation going during the questions would you mind trying something for me? Spend at least one minute on each question before you move on. It may feel forced at first, but think of a way to reword it or share a personal story that may encourage more kids to participate. I think this could really help keep the boys focused and engaged with what you are saying. Before you know it, small group time will be over and you'll have had a great conversation with your boys!"

No one wants to be berated for something they are volunteering to do. Our teams will be much more receptive to our constructive criticism when we let them know how proud we are of them and how much we appreciate them.

While I'm on this topic, I'm going to share with you an idea that was given to me at the Northwest Ministry Conference a couple of years ago. The speaker shared her struggle with busyness in ministry and finding balance. One thing that helped her get back on track on Mondays was to write thank you cards to three of her volunteers. She included specifics like "I saw you get down on Jack's level to listen to his story about his baseball game this weekend. I appreciate your genuine interest in the kids' lives!" This not only encouraged her team, but it helped her be on the lookout for the positive things instead of only the things that went wrong.

I started doing this with all of my volunteers, but it is my youth team that seems to appreciate the personal notes the most. When I started at my church, one of the first cards I wrote ended up on the Instagram account of one of my student leaders. He was excited about serving and was thankful I recognized his hard work. It is such a simple thing to do, but it means the world to my team.

CONCLUSION

Empower. Equip. Encourage.

Doing these three things well is not easy, but they form the key to raising up young leaders. Can you have one without the others? Sure, but I don't believe it works nearly as well. You can encourage without empowering, but that only goes so far. And empowering someone but not equipping them properly is just a recipe for disaster. In order to have a truly healthy ministry and strong youth leaders, you must commit to all three.

I don't claim to have this whole thing figured out. In fact, most of the things I have written about here are things I'm still trying to implement. I have a long way to go and a lot to learn, but I do know this: Your investment in the lives of your student leaders will pay off in your ministry and in their lives.

We don't know exactly how old Timothy was when Paul mentored him, but he was young enough that Paul had to remind him to not allow others to look down on him because of it.[75] Your student leaders need to know that they can be used by God to share his love and his Word. Every single person has a part to play in his Kingdom, whether they're twelve or a hundred and twelve.

114

Can we have an honest moment here? Working with teenagers is hard. It takes a lot of work and a lot of energy. Implementing these suggestions may not reap immediate rewards, but I will tell you that the long-term benefits far outweigh the present cost. We are investing in the lives of these young people, both in their physical leadership development and also in their spiritual walk with the Lord.

Nelson Searcy writes, "The truth is, when people serve, they become more like Jesus."[76] Inviting our student leaders to step up is doing more than just handing them greater responsibility—it is welcoming them into a deeper and more meaningful relationship with Christ.

REFLECTION QUESTIONS

1. Do I have any reservations about giving student leaders more responsibility? Why?
2. Which of these three areas should I focus on improving?
3. What am I doing to invest in the lives of my student leaders?
4. What are some service elements I can delegate to our youth leaders?
5. Who are five students I should approach about getting involved in children's ministry?

END OF CHAPTER NOTES

[74] Celestine Chua, "How to Give Constructive Criticism: 6 Helpful Tips," *Personal Excellence*, http://personalexcellence.co/blog/constructive-criticism/ (accessed October 2, 2015).

[75] 1 Timothy 4:12

[76] Nelson Searcy and Jennifer Dykes Henson, *Connect: How to Double Your Number of Volunteers* (Grand Rapids, Mich.: Baker Books, 2012).

6.2 DESIGNING YOUR
SPECIAL EVENTS CALENDAR
Dorene Heeter

It's time to create your annual ministry calendar and decide what events to add and which to remove. As you sit in front of a blank calendar, you realize that this just might be one of the most stressful times of the year (outside of creating your budget)! Truth be told, your calendar and budget are very closely connected, in that they affect each other. Planning annual calendars can be exciting and stressful for both the detail-oriented person and the organizationally challenged individual. With careful planning and sharing of resources from the colleagues you network with, your next event and annual calendar can be a success.

Every fall in the Pacific Northwest, our church begins to plan what we believe God wants to see accomplished in our church and our community. The children's ministry team I serve and have the privilege to lead will gather and prayerfully, creatively, and intentionally plan out our coming year. We then actively seek for ways to improve or change what we have done in order to accomplish the mission of God and our church.

Serving as a children's pastor (one year as a youth pastor) for over twenty-six years, I have had the opportunity to be a part of a range of churches. Each of these had distinctive qualities; from very large churches, a church plant that met weekly in a theater, a church of less than a hundred people, and currently a mid-size church of about four hundred.

Calendar planning in each of these scenarios has given me a unique perspective and the ability to adapt. I've been married to my best friend for almost twenty-five years and I am the proud mother of two great young men, currently ages fifteen and eighteen. Throughout my twenty-six years of experience in the ministry, I have learned how to effectively plan and juggle our home, school, and ministry calendars. My approach to the ministry calendar started out as a survival skill. I am happy to say, that after a bit of experience, that it has become one of the most effective ways for me to lead the church. I am excited to share with you some tools that I have learned; hopefully, they will aid you in your events and calendar planning.

The first part in planning an effective calendar is to identify your goal that you wish to achieve by the end of the year.

WHAT IS YOUR GOAL?

Begin with prayer, because God has a purpose for your children and families, and the events you put on the calendar play a large role in that. Follow his leading and direction. Consider also the stated mission and written values of your church; these often are developed by your lead pastor or pastoral team. If you don't know them, seek your lead pastor out and learn his heart and the direction he feels God is leading the church. You need to know what specifically you want to accomplish with each event, stick to that purpose, and carefully prepare the environment so that purpose gets accomplished.

Will This Be Inward or Outward Focused?

Bring clarity to your events by sharing their true purpose. Ask yourself if this event is for those inside your church, outside your church, or both? Is the purpose of the event to unite families and fellowship? Will this be a community outreach event? Know your target, know your audience, and find the best way to communicate this to your teams.

What Is The Main Event?

One of the current trends for children's leaders is to strategically place the greatest emphasis for events on the Sunday morning church experience for kids and only place a few midweek or repeating events outside of the weekend. Sunday, after all, is the "bread and butter" of ministry. It is where many children's ministries funnel their energy, finances and people resources. We have found great success by hosting Invite Days during our Sunday morning children's ministries. "Invite Day" is our term to let our kids (and parents) know that this is a special day when they can invite their friends to church and know that we have something super-cool planned so they want to bring them.

Yes, I know, you already have pretty amazing Sunday morning services planned; I don't question that. But kids love the excitement of something new and hey, wouldn't you want to come check out "Mustache Mania" or "Silly Band Sunday" or "Crazy Hat Day"? Kids eat this up! I know of a local church that successfully hosts a special event fifty-two Sundays a year! (I understand if you don't believe me. In conjunction with these guest-friendly and outward-focused events, we communicate to our kids the importance of being an "inviter" and "includer." We remind them that we are on a mission from God and that these events are fun fishers-of-men "bait" to help them reach out to their friends and family.

WHAT ARE THE "BIG ROCKS"?

Our senior pastor likes to call the most important and main church calendar items our "Big Rocks." They are the ones that must be prioritized if they are to succeed in your ministry setting. Decide and plan the *non-negotiables* of children's ministries that God has called you and your team to do, for example, Sunday morning kids' churches, nursery, clubs, kids' camp, discipleship courses, kids' water baptism class, small groups, parenting classes, baby dedications, outreaches (VBS, Harvest Festival, Jingle Jam, etc.).

WHAT SEASON IS IT?

You may have already discovered by now that there are definite seasons in ministry just as there are seasons of the year. If you have ever stood on a ladder then know what it's like to look at a place from a higher vantage point. It is amazing how often you can see new things with just a slight increase in elevation. The same thing is true about looking out of a window in a tall building. Perhaps you have taken a plane flight and stared down below at your own neighborhood. It is fun to be able to pick out landmarks and other features that are undistinguishable from the ground level. In the same way, we need to view our ministries from various altitudes. The organization of your children's ministry looks different when you start to distance yourself from it. You can see more, and can see how each event relates to others on an annual, instead of weekly, scale. When planning your specific ministry calendar you will need to rise above a fifty-foot level and take a look at the bigger picture to identify when to add things and when to slow things down. Consider these different perspectives:

50-foot level. This regards your *children's ministry calendar and events*. It views your ministry individually, apart from the church. This affords you a fifty-two-week snapshot of the events and activities initiated by you and your team. Consider how closely things are scheduled, and if they even overlap with one another. It is not uncommon to see conflicting events scheduled within a single ministry. Tailoring your schedule according to this perspective should help you establish a good rhythm for your church.

100-foot level. This is what we call the *you and your family* perspective. This perspective allows you to integrate the commitments and demands of your own family *in addition* to your children's ministry calendar. Remember, each gain in altitude incorporates other scheduling factors; it does not eliminate other things. Have you left enough room to cultivate a healthy marriage or single life? Do you have kids? Have you been honest about the amount of time they will need of you as it relates to school, sports, or other extracurricular events? What about your own personal health? Is there enough time for you to sleep, eat well, or exercise? Use this perspective to help you schedule matters according to your personal perspective.

150-foot level. Now it is time to factor in *volunteers and parents*. All too often we overschedule the families of our church. Remember that most people have multiple kids, and that they want to support each child equally. Our programs often divide families across multiple evenings and activities. Do your best to synchronize your ministry for the entire family. You must also protect your volunteers. The Pareto Principle, better known as the 80/20 Rule, suggests that 20 percent of your volunteers will produce 80 percent of your work.[77] Guard this core group and be careful not to overschedule or ask too much of them.

250-foot level. At this level we increase our perspective significantly. Now it is time to incorporate the schedule of you *pastoral team and board*. This is a team perspective and will require you to begin to make compromises. This is the first level of scheduling where other people have more influence over your calendar than you do. Be prepared to be gracious and flexible. You may be asked to shift days off or entire vacation plans. You may be asked to spend extra time at the church for meetings or reports. Know that these are often very important. Change what you can, and be a team player when asked. That is not to say that there is no room for pushback here. Your lead pastor needs to know if you feel too busy, or if you are unable to provide the support that your family needs. Too many team events will begin to limit the amount of ministry you will be able to do. Integrating the team perspective into your annual calendar is very important.

1,000-foot level. This perspective is the *holistic church view* and considers multi-ministry and mission perspectives. This is the most complex and difficult perspective to integrate. Most churches struggle to ever develop, or even consider developing a 1,000-foot view of the ministry calendar. Even on a "big events" level this can be difficult. It requires the entire team to selflessly consider the goals, families, staff, and mission of the church. This is also the place where you will be asked to make the greatest sacrifices on behalf of your ministry. Don't get defensive or territorial. Remember that children's ministry is one that touches nearly every other ministry of the church. You may have to do the most work in order to shape your ministry model in a way that serves your church.

After taking into account the perspectives of each level and asking for wisdom from colleagues and leaders, you next need to look at the timing of the event. Ask: Is this too close to our last event? Does this event overshadow or conflict with a "big rock"? Is this a time to move ahead? Rest? Regroup? Will this burn out myself or my volunteers? Is this the right time or will it cause me to neglect my family due to overscheduling?

Once you have prayed, determined the focus for each item and/or event on the calendar, noted where the "big rocks" of your church are placed, and examined the season your church and team are in, plan away and dream big! Keith Tusing follows a simple model to help evaluate the most important things, or "big rocks" of his ministry. He says that you must:

1. Determine your vision, mission, and values.
2. Write down your goals for this year.
3. Evaluate your resources.
4. Determine which events best accomplish your mission and goals.
5. Assemble a calendar team—get input.
6. Review and refine—evaluate and realign.[78]

Have You Planned For Fun?

Social events and seasonal celebrations must not be overlooked. To build morale, your team must have fun together. Staff meetings and curriculum planning are a priority, but parties, outings, activities, and seasonal celebrations build memories and "team glue" that pay huge dividends long term. These fun activities are best when planned to fit the overall long-term schedules.

Communicate With Parents

Communication with parents is a huge factor in your long-term success. Parent meetings, eyeball-to-eyeball, are important and should be put on your calendar. These could be potluck dinners on a rehearsal night or at separate times that fit your schedules. I recommend two or three parent meetings per year. (We have two Sunday morning services and I utilize the first service to host the meeting, encouraging our parents to worship in the second service.) We call these meetings "Parent Preview," and just as the title suggests we are giving them a preview of what's new and coming for the next six months to a year, additionally, we celebrate them as parents and give them one to two parenting tools for their toolbox to help them be the spiritual leaders of their homes. Each time we host this event we present another tool and/or resource for them.

Children's Ministries Magazine released an article, "Exclusive Research: The State of Family Ministry," which detailed parents' responses when they asked parents to rank the tools they find most helpful to train their children spiritually.[79] The main point of that article, written by the Christine Yount Jones, the executive editor of *Children's Ministry Magazine,* is: "How can we as primary encouragers of parents in their quest to train their children become their biggest fans? Parents are grateful for what you do week in and week out. They recognize that you bring a level of faith-building expertise to their children's faith journeys that they couldn't on their own. They look to you to believe in them, cheer for them, equip them, communicate with them, and walk alongside them to help their children have a growing relationship with Jesus!"

Partnering with parents is a key to successful children's ministries. I recommend putting these meetings as a priority on your calendar and planning your other events around them.

How to Plan and Execute Large Events

Basic timelines will help you and your team to accomplish events in bite-size chunks. It is a great tool that can empower others to serve, because everyone can see the overall execution plan, and assignments can be given. Curriculum companies have mastered large event planning and I have used their templates for our own timeline planning. After you have written out the why and the what for your event, recruit your team, create a timeline and outline assignments. Don't forget to include team meetings in your timeline, so you can follow-up on the assignments and continue to mark off your checklists. When the team collaborates and can see the progress, momentum and excitement is built. The team will "own" the event and you will all share in its success!

The most important thing is to create a plan that other people can follow. The easiest way to make sure people are with you is to create a plan in the company of others. Set some time aside and invite your core leaders to help you draft a plan of attack for you next event. Write things down and do whatever you can to be clear. Job descriptions, due dates, and material lists will all be helpful in the execution of a large event. Also helpful—a vivid imagination. Put yourself in the shoes of a teacher, host, or security personnel. What will they need? Where will they need it? Hindsight is good, but foresight is best. Do what you can to anticipate the environments you want to create and what it will take to turn those ideas into reality.

WHY EVALUATE AND MAKE CHANGES?

Each and every event should be evaluated, no matter how big or small. Ask your team to share the "wins" so you can celebrate together and with the congregation. Don't forget to take pictures or video at your events and recruit a photographer and/or videographer to do this; you won't have time or remember since you are leading the event. Ask your team to give input by sharing the "misses" of the event. This would be the ways to improve it or even continue it for next year. Don't shy away from input and invite the gift of constructive criticism. It will make for a better event and help make you a better leader, personally growing through your leadership style and build trust in the eyes of your team. A leader who invites collaboration and input (especially when some things don't go as planned) establishes confidence and stability on their team.

It's important to consistently evaluate your ministry events. Kara Powell and Chap Clark describe a process where three key questions are asked: (1) How are we doing in this area? (2) What are our strengths? (3) What are our weaknesses and opportunities for growth?[80] After answering these three essential questions, they argue that leaders should figure out which events to keep, end, or start from scratch. Find a way to evaluate your ministry events in a way that can be compared year after year. This allows you to track progress over time and make substantial improvements to your overall strategy.

In order to be truly effective, you can't just plan. You have to open each event up to honest evaluation.

SUMMARY

We covered a lot of information in this chapter. Let's review how you can plan, schedule, and execute special events in your children's ministry. First, remember to pray and ask God's help. He will give you the direction, creativity and vision. Second, determine your goal and establish the purpose for the event. Third, think through the big rocks of your church and the season you are in by taking a look from 50- to 1,000-foot levels, and take both into consideration before placing items on the calendar. Fourth, don't forget to plan for fun and communicate to parents. Last, plan away and dream big! But never forget to evaluate and make changes if the same event makes your top ten for next year.

REFLECTION QUESTIONS

1. What is the first thing you should do before you start brainstorming and writing down calendar dates?

2. Who can help you network with to help you navigate event ideas or planning or find resources?

3. Do you know the "big rocks" of your church? Do you know the mission and values of your church? These will help you to plan and act as a filter for all the brainstormed ideas that don't fit into the mission of your church.

4. Where can you put on the calendar some fun for your team and for your own children?

5. Do you have a plan in place or a system to keep communication channels open and flowing with parents?

END OF CHAPTER NOTES

[77] Greg McKeown, *Essentialism: The Disciplined Pursuit of Less* (New York: Crown Business, 2014).

[78] Keith Tusing, "Creating the Annual Ministry Calendar," *Cmbuzx.com*, November 17, 2015, http://cmbuzz.com/2011/10/planning-the-childrens-ministry-annual-calendar/.

[79] Christine Yount Jones, "Exclusive Research: The State of Family Ministry," *Children's Ministry*, http://childrensministry.com/articles/exclusive-research-state-family-ministry/ (accessed October 2, 2015).

[80] Kara E. Powell, Chap Clark, John Ortberg and Jim Candy, *Sticky Faith: Everyday Ideas to Build Lasting Faith in Your Kids* (Grand Rapids, Mich: Zondervan, 2011).

6.3 BEING HEARD IN A NOISY WORLD
Monica Bowsher and Brent Colby

Communication is a critical part of your children's ministry strategy. No ministry succeeds without effective and consistent communication between the leadership, volunteers, parents, and kids. You must break down complex ideas and convey them to a variety of people on a daily basis. Think about it: The success of your volunteer rotations, special events, and discipleship depend on your ability to communicate effectively. But you are not the only one trying to communicate with your audience. You have more competition than ever for the attention of the people in your church. We live in a noisy world and it is more difficult than ever to be heard.

We have good news and bad news. The good news is that you have access to more tools to get your message across to people. The bad news is that everyone now has equal access to these tools. For example: phone calls, text messages, and social networks are a great way to connect with people. This is why every school, corporation, and charity has adopted them as primary means of communication. What can you do to cut through cereal ads, PTA meetings, and fund-raising campaigns to get through to your families? It may be easier than you think.

We are going to suggest three things to you. If you can follow them, then you will not be drowned out by the noise of the world around you. First, you need to pick a set of communication tools. You don't have time to use everything, so pick a few that will give you the biggest bang for your buck. Second, you need to make sure that your message is personal. People like you more than they like your brand. Third, and this point is critical, you have to make your message memorable. Do something, anything that will help your message stick with your audience. Finally you need to develop the habit of repeating yourself. Groups of people don't start picking up your message until you are usually sick of saying it. Our last point is that you need to repeat yourself again.

SHARPEN YOUR PENCIL

Identify your communication tools and modes. Figure out which tools you will become excellent at and which ones you will ignore. Do you prefer writing with a pen or pencil? I (Brent) like pens: they don't need to be sharpened and write well on most types of paper. But I always carry a pencil in my bag. Because I like to sketch, a pencil is often the right tool for the job. I use both a pen and a pencil to communicate. When I communicate in words I use a pen. When I communicate with images I use a pencil. I never carry chalk; chalk makes me sneeze.

You have an incredible number of choices to make when it comes to communication tools. We're not just talking about mediums such as social networks, emails, or printed material. We're talking about *types* social networks, emails, or printed materials. The church of yesterday only had a few tools to choose from; but you have thousands. It is impossible for you to become good at all of them, so you must choose a few. How many is "a few"? A few might be three, but a few may be more than that for you. It depends on how much time and prior expertise you have to invest into communication. Your first job is to pick the communication tools that best suit you and your ministry.

How do you choose the best tools? Good question. Ask yourself what your natural communication skills look like. Are you a charismatic speaker and do you own a video camera? Perhaps you should consider posting videos online. Are you articulate and do you know how to write? Consider sending out a weekly email or keeping a ministry blog. Can you use Photoshop? Perhaps you should be designing and communicating through the visual arts. Figuring out what tool is best for you requires a little introspection. Ask people on your team what your strengths are. It may be more difficult for you to choose which tools *not* to use. When the next social network comes out you must resist investing lots of time into it. If you have limited time and still want to be an effective communicator then you may have to ignore it entirely. Be disciplined—those other tools are dead to you.

There is a difference between communication *tools* and *modes*. A tool is a particular device: Twitter, Facebook, or Morse code. Your mode describes how you will utilize these tools: Once a day? Every Sunday? On a submarine? An effective strategy must also describe how you intend to use the tools you have chosen. It is essential that you become consistent! Twelve monthly videos will have a greater impact than twelve daily videos. Your fortnight of vlogging will be forgotten before . . . wait, what are talking about? Nothing—and that is the point.

Effective modes of communication have the same shape and are released at consistent intervals. If you release a monthly email update to your church families then it must come out every month. It must also contain similar types and amounts of content. This is what I mean when I say *shape*. People hear you better when they know what to expect from you. That is not to say that you can't surprise them. But it is to say that you must be consistent in both what you say and how often you say it.

OK, you have picked the tools that you will to use and the tools that you will ignore. You have also established a pattern for how these tools will be used. Good. Now let's look at some guidelines for communicating with people.

MAKE IT PERSONAL

People don't want to hear from your robot, they want to hear from you. If you want to become an effective communicator then you must learn how to make your communication personal. Relying on automated modes of communication will greatly reduce the amount of people who hear you. You can make your communication personal on two levels. The first level is that of your audience. The second level of personalization comes down to you and *your* voice.

There is a magic word that everyone wants to hear. It is powerful and has done more to move people to action than any other word in the human language. This word transcends social, economic, and geographical boundaries. It works on children as well as adults. It is particularly effective with people you don't know. What is that word? That word is Dave. Well, that word is Dave if your name is Dave. If your name is Jamie, however, that word is Jamie. You see what I am doing here? The most effective thing you can do when communicating with an individual is to use his or her name. This is not always possible. The next best thing is to address a select group of people. "Hey, Saturday Volunteers" is much more effective than, "To Whom it May Concern." Dan Zarrella combed through millions of emails sent through a marketing service to determine which ones got opened, read, or deleted. He discovered that communication that is able to utilize people's names had the greatest effect on its audiences. [81] Not just any name, the name of the person you are talking to. This is even truer when you are having a personal conversation with someone. Whenever you can, address your audience as specifically as possible. Their ears will perk up and you will have bought an opportunity to gain their attention.

Authenticity is a critical part of personality. People smell a gimmick from a mile away and they distrust them.[82] Sincere communication resonates with others; it is trustworthy. My husband, James and I (Monica) return to our favorite restaurant time and time again. The menu is simple, the prices are fair, and the service is consistently awesome. We don't go there because of the promotions, gimmicks, or street-corner sign-flippers. We go there because the staff goes out of their way to make a personal connection with us. The same thing is true about the messages you send to the families in your church. People listen to you because they trust you and have a relationship with you. They don't listen to you because you are a slick salesperson with a deal they can't refuse.

IT'S HALFTIME GAME TIME

It is important that your message be memorable, like the half-time ads at the Super Bowl. If you don't know what the Super Bowl is then let us describe it to you: it is a primetime television event where corporations play ads between spurts of American football. Cats, bikinis, and puppies spur thousands to go out and buy dog food, web domains, and cases of Budweiser. These ads have been designed to stick in your brain. They are funny, smart and emotional. You are not in the dog food business, you're in the Jesus business. Thousands of kids and parents are counting on you to share messages that are hard to forget.

Chip and Dan Heath have developed a formula for those trying to make memorable or "sticky" messages. They tell people to make their messages simple, unexpected, concrete, credible, emotional, and story-oriented.[83] You should read their book, but let us summarize the big idea for you here: Your message must deliver the right content in a clear and fun way.

Don't try to say too much. People can only take away a few bits of information at a time. Your ten-point take-home flyer has to go. Say less to increase the number of people who hear you. Granted, it is hard to shave down your messages; there is so much information that people need to know! Just make sure that the vehicle you are using to drive home information matches the road you are on. Many of us drive a tank down bicycle paths when we send home a pile of papers, flyers, and art projects. If you are on a narrow avenue, your tank of an info-dump is going to have little or no impact. When you can match the vehicle to the path, say a simple postcard or sticker, your voice will be heard. When one of your kids comes home with a smiley face from school, it says more than her teacher could ever convey in a daily one-page write-up.

Appeal to the human side of others. That is right: share things that appeal to people's feelings, wants, or desires. Celebrate good news with happy words. Share concerns with sad words. Express concerns with . . . you get the idea. And don't just limit your expressions to words. Go ahead and use entire stories as well.

People remember the emotional investment that you have put into your messages.

PETE AND REPEAT

Pete and Repeat were in a boat. Pete fell out, who was left? Repeat.

If you are not tired of saying it, then your audience hasn't heard you. Patrick Lencioni calls this approach *overcommunication*[84]; we call it being borderline annoying. You have to repeat critical things over, and over again. Some say that you must repeat a message seven times before it begins to stick.[85] Seven times! So often we feel that our job is over the second we send the email, hang the poster, or mail the flyer. The secret to effective communication is that you have to do it over and over and over again. Not only that, you have to say the same thing in a variety of ways.

Earlier you chose a few communication tools. You will concentrate on these tools to get your message across. Know that you will have to use all of these tools multiple times in order to be heard in this noisy world. Forget video announcement, think video announcements! I have an event coming up in our ministry where we scheduled no fewer than seven weeks of video announcements. You have to do the same thing in your church. Realize that repeating a message has the greatest effect over time. You can't shout, "camp, camp, camp, camp, camp, camp, camp!" in front of a group of parents and consider your job done. You must spread your communication out over time before in order to get your message across.

ONE LAST THING

You have a lot to think about and that it can be overwhelming. Pick one thing from this chapter that stood out to you and get to work. Perhaps you are using too many or too few communication tools. Maybe you need to work on your overcommunication. It's possible that you are starting to sound like a used car salesmen when promoting your ministry events. You can do it; you can be heard in this noisy world. Master one component before moving on to the next. This is one area of your ministry that can't wait for you to develop a more effective strategy.

REFLECTION QUESTIONS

1. What are your three main communication tools? Which ones must you stay away from because they waste your time?
2. How can you be more personal in your communication? How are people connecting with you in your communication?
3. What is something that you can do to make your communication more simple and funny?
4. How will you communicate the same message multiple times? Can you put this strategy down on paper with precise dates?

END OF CHAPTER NOTES

[81] Dan Zarrella, *Zarrella's Hierarchy of Contagiousness: The Science, Design, and Engineering of Contagious Ideas,* published by Amazon/Do You Zoom, The Domino Project, 2011).

[82] Simon Sinek, *Start with Why: How Great Leaders Inspire Everyone to Take Action* (New York: Portfolio, 2011).

[83] Chip Heath and Dan Heath, *Made to Stick: Why Some Ideas Survive and Others Die* (New York: Random House, 2007).

[84] Patrick M. Lencioni, *The Advantage: Why Organizational Health Trumps Everything Else In Business* (San Francisco: Jossey-Bass, 2012).

[85] Lencioni, p. 141.

6.4 FARSIGHTED CHILDREN'S MINISTRY
Nick Caalim

Recently I got some bad news. In reality, it's some news that has been creeping up on me for some time now but I decided to ignore that it's true. Only a few months ago (OK, it was six years) I turned thirty, and life totally changed. Almost instantly my slacks began the process of slowly shrinking around the waist. But that wasn't the worst part of it. The worst part was that I began to not be able to see. Almost overnight I had to start wearing glasses. I have to wear glasses so the things I read on a page or screen aren't too blurry. I need a little help getting those letters and pictures to become clear. Yup, vision problems. I get a little envious sometimes when people can just look at their phone checking Instagram or whatever without having to fumble around for their glasses first.

The eye doctor tells me I have hyperopia, which sounds kinda cool. I've known I'm a pretty hyper guy my entire life, but really all it means is I'm farsighted. I can see things better when they are farther away. Things are just more clear. The glasses help with that.

The glasses I rummage around for every morning just to see what time it is help make clear what looks blurry up close.

Farsightedness is an issue many people deal with. And it's also a problem with which most schools, community groups and churches struggle. You'll hear the evidence all the time. You'll hear folks calling out the battle cry: "children are our future," encouraging others to get active in preparing for a better tomorrow. Even churches with amazing children's programs fall prey to being farsighted. And really, most churches are the most farsighted of all. I clearly remember standing on the stage at our church, with quite a number of people in the crowd before me, proudly declaring, "we must impact today's children because our future depends on it!"

The best way to say it is all too often we simply have a better, clearer vision of what our children can be in the future when they are grown up. Which is a problem—a big problem. We are missing it big time.

But there is an alternative. Rather than living with farsightedness, we can put on some corrective lenses and develop a different perspective. We can, and ought to, develop nearsightedness. Let's gain a clearer picture of what is, and can be right now. Let's seek God's insight on what impact this young generation can have right now.

LEAD

Let's explore three ways you can *lead* others to develop nearsightedness for the children in your world: Lead your team to *strengthen* their children's ministry perspective. Lead parents to *develop* a nearsighted vision of their children. And lead your kids in an *empowering* message and call to action.

As a leader of children's ministry you have a unique role. So much of it is a duality. With the mastery of a tightrope walker, you must often learn to balance between opposites. You are fun, and serious. You build structure around what naturally is chaos. You act with purpose but have to be highly reactive to the needs and demands that surround you. And, probably the most difficult to keep in balance, you must be both present and future. Undoubtedly there is pressure to have a program, environment, or culture that excites children to return. So we focus on doing what will engage the kids for the here and now. However, we want to also have sustainability in mind. There is the pressure of building something that prepares the kids for the long haul. We don't want to be the reason our church has a short future or limited lifespan.

This perspective can lend itself to being overcome by fear. We begin to question and revisit every decision we make, become overly critical of ourselves and others, and ultimately weaken our resolve that what we are doing really matters. To be totally honest I've asked myself a few times why I do certain lessons, or "Why am I doing yet another altar call where every hand goes up? Is this lesson stuff sticking? Will they even remember?" I can't be the only one who has ever had a thought like these slip through my brain. Maybe I am . . . because I'm sure you are all saints. After all, you're reading a nice Christian book on children's ministry, as only saints would.

BACK TO THE FUTURE

It has been my personal experience for the eyes of children's ministers to brighten when they gain the first glimpse of becoming more nearsighted. Plainly, your team gets stronger, and feels more on mission when they know their effort is focused on the now-ness of the kids.

I'll just say it. I can't stand it when people call children "our future," What?! Are they not part of our world now? I nearly drove my car off the side of the road when I saw a reader board stating, "School—a building with four walls and a future inside." It makes me want to scream. I get it. . . . I know many of these children will outlive me, and thus they are going to be around in "the future." I get that. My problem isn't about the space-time continuum and how things lineup through history.

When we call them "the future" we imply they must wait their turn. We imply a message such as:

- "You are not yet."
- "Continue to prepare. Your turn is coming."
- "We've got this for now. But just wait, you'll have your chance."
- "What you can add isn't valuable just yet, but give it time, and it'll matter later."

Kids are not the future generation; they are a young generation. "Future" means it isn't yet here, but let me tell you—they're here. They're hard to miss. And they're awesome.

I get slightly more (and by slightly I actually mean a *whole lot* more) irritated when people call our children's ministries the church of the future. *What?!* What does that mean? They aren't a part of the body of Christ because they can't grow facial hair? They don't have a driver's license? They don't make enough money in allowance to fill the offering plates? Let's be honest about this. When did Jesus say you had to be a certain age to follow him? Jesus welcomed little ones to himself, and set them up as the example of what we all should strive for in faith.

I know I'm preaching to the choir here. You know how important what we do is. But let me challenge you on *why* you think it is important. The future of our congregation depends on having the future generation ready to take the lead, right? (I'm really hoping you didn't just say a hearty "Amen" and highlight that last sentence.) That last statement has truth to it. Without an heir an empire comes to an end. But that thinking is pure farsightedness. We are missing it if that is the only picture we are able to see.

It is possible to have a vision of *them* for now, not only for their future. Nearsightedness looks see what living for Jesus looks like at eight years old, and four years old, and eleven. We need to start working with the Now in mind. Don't let them miss out on sixteen years of impacting their world because you only have a picture of what they can do as an eighteen-year-old. Can you even imagine the confidence they will build? Can you fathom the fortitude of their faith?

As the leader, get a vision for yourself. Let that vision inspire you. Help your people see that vision by explaining it to them plainly. Just describe it to them. Nurture it within them. Let this nurtured vision inspire them. You'll experience a breath of fresh air in your leadership. You'll see how this invigorates and strengthens your team.

Look Closely

Secondly, in developing nearsightedness for today's children, children's ministry leaders must lead parents to develop a nearsighted vision of their own children. Any parent knows that when we look at our kids sometimes all we see is the growing list of "to do" items that has to be accomplished to maintain their health, safety, and success in life (not to mention our own sanity). All we see sometimes is the struggle of parenting. Our current reality of raising children can be exhausting. It seems more encouraging to fantasize about the future when they are grown and taking care of themselves. Focusing on the future, in many ways, is preferred. But we must not fall prey to this temptation. We can't forfeit these years, simply working hard and waiting it out until graduation or just beyond. Making the most of these young years starts with having a clear of vision of how God can use them right now.

No one knows your children better than you, the parent. You know what makes them click, what energizes or upsets them, what they love, and even how they think. Take all this into consideration as you develop a nearsighted vision for your kids. God made them who they are on purpose. It's not an accident they act the way they do. So let's use that uniqueness to set our kids up for their greatest success right now. Proverbs 22:6 (NIV) gives us a great promise; "Start children off on the way they should go, and even when they are old they will not turn from it." This gives me hope about their future. But it means I need to be careful to make sure I've discovered the way *they* should go. Their path may not be the same as my path. The way my youngest child may need to be "started off on the way," is probably different than the way my older child did. This requires a huge amount of attentiveness to the personality and spiritual climate of our children's hearts and our homes.

The first step to parents developing a clear nearsighted vision to what Jesus wants to do in and through their children is simply acknowledging Jesus is at work in them right now. Be attentive to it. Get on board with it. And look for ways to set them up to use their unique personality, gifts and experiences today, this weekend, and now.

I hear these statements being said by parents who have a nearsighted vision for their kids:

- "You are so good at art, let's use that gift to make a card for our neighbor."
- "I'm so glad God gave me a child who has such a loving heart for the kids who don't have many friends"
- "Before you start soccer practice let's ask Jesus to help you use that amazing talent to praise him."

CALLED TO ACTION

Lastly, your role as a children's leader calls you to lead your kids with an empowering message and a call to action. This idea has changed the way I talk to children, and how I ask them to respond to Jesus' love. I used to call the kids to receive Jesus into their lives so they can be with Him in Heaven. But now I've changed. Jesus offers us abundant life which can begin right now. Jesus called his disciples and they immediately followed him. This can be the same for our kids today. The fruit of the Spirit can begin growing in their life right away. It's never too early to allow the Holy Spirit to work, guide, and form the lives of these children. Their journey and adventure begin now.

I spend much of my teaching opportunities in front of children encouraging them to use the gifts and talents they have to spread the love of Jesus to their friends, family, neighbors, and people at school. This typically is followed by a "you don't have to wait until you have a driver's license" phrase. In the same way Jesus used the lunch of a little boy to feed thousands, Jesus can use whatever we offer him to do miracles that touch many. I'd imagine the kids get a bit weary of me continuing this message throughout the year, but continual reminders, constant prodding, are important (how many times do I have to tell my kids to pick up their shoes before they do it, and that's a pretty easy task to do. Reminders are good.).

It's important to keep what we are asking the kids to do "bite-sized." Shoot . . . it's hard to get adults to invite their adult friends to church, even. I've been known to get pretty descriptive in explaining how kids can carry out a call to action. The more they can imagine them themselves making an impact, the better they can see themselves taking action. We've even done practice in preparation for a large event! While many adults were being trained for altar response, we held similar training for kids. We knew kids would respond at the event as well as adults, so we wanted to have kids ready to receive them. The training and practice built confidence, took the initial anxiety out of it, and allowed the kids to see how it plays out in reality. The night of the event when people swarmed to the response area, tears filled my eyes as I watched the kids I'd worked with lead these kids they didn't even know toward Jesus. We had led them in bite-sized steps to a pretty big moment.

And we can never encourage them enough. We constantly speak truth over their lives, continually reminding them of their place in the Kingdom of God. We remember that Jesus said some pretty outlandish things to encourage his disciples. For example: "Very truly I tell you, whoever believes in me will do the works I have been doing, and they will do even greater things than these" (John 14:12, NIV). What? Do even greater things than Jesus did? That sounds pretty absurd. But Jesus said it!

We can never speak enough life and truth over these kids. I hear these words being spoken:

- "Don't feel like you can do it? You can do all things through Christ who gives you strength."
- "Feeling too afraid? God didn't give you a spirit of fear, but of courage."
- "The way God made you, your gifts and talents are the exact things He needed in place for you to change the world."

Michael was a fourth-grade boy in our children's church. He came nearly every weekend. He was a guest of Ms. Ann. The faithful, loving, and saintly Ms. Ann would drive over to the apartment complex of some old family friends and pick up the kids who wanted to go to church. Michael was one of them. I've never met Michael's parents or anyone from Michael's family. Ms. Ann made sure there was a place in her van for him, or she'd just make two trips.

And did we ever get to know Michael. Over and over again, the team of leaders at kids' church would spend one-on-one time trying to get Michael to behave less disruptively. Or encouraging him that, in fact, the stuff we are talking about really is interesting. That's just saying it nicely—man, was he ever a headache sometimes. Then we began noticing a trend. While many of the kids Ms. Ann brought would come and go, Michael was pretty consistent. I thought that was just because the other kids chose to stay at home and sleep in rather than go with Ms Ann, or they'd moved, or something else. And he brought friends.

"This your friend, Michael?"

"Oh yeah. . . . He wanted to come today. He's not in my grade, but can he sit with me?"

"Sure . . . glad you're both here."

If this or a similar conversation happened once, it happened a hundred times.

"Hey Michael, you sure do have a lot of kids that come with you and Ms. Ann."

"Well, they need to be here." With a shrug of a shoulder, Michael walked on by and sat down. Then like a bolt of lightning it dawned on me: Ms. Ann is the chauffer here, the catalyst for these kids coming, but actually Michael is the one bringing them. This kid, who had given me a fair share of gray hairs, had figured it out way before me. Michael had a different perspective than I had at the time. Michael is Now.

I'm Now

Kids everywhere are saying, "I'm Now." They show us that they are ready when they pray, when they serve, and when they give. Unfortunately kids are sold a lie that says their Now-ness kicks in as they get older. Innocently, how many times do we ask our little ones, "What do you want to be when you grow up?" I imagine that 99 percent of high school graduation speeches include some kind of phrasing where the guest speaker commissions the graduating class to go make their imprint on the world.

A nearsighted children's leader see that the kids are not only the future—they are Now. A nearsighted children's leader has a clear picture of the impact a child can make on his or her part of the world. A nearsighted children's leader knows that a child's faith, hope and belief in Jesus can be every bit as strong as any adult's, and usually stronger. Nearsighted children's leaders don't exert all their energy for the idea that we need to prepare now for a strong church tomorrow. A nearsighted children's leader sees the gifts and talents in the lives of this young generation and sees how they can be used now.

Lean in and hear them say it in hushed tones. Stand back and watch them act it out in big ways. Whatever you do, don't make them wait. Teach them to say it louder. Help them show it on purpose. Rally them to stand up and declare "I'm Now!"

REFLECTION QUESTIONS

1. What perspective do you and the people on your children's ministry team lead with? Is it farsighted? Or nearsighted?
2. In what ways will you help your team develop a clear vision of who and what your kids can do right now?
3. Parents, ask yourselves, "What is the spiritual fruit I see in my children?"
4. What is God's Word of truth specifically for the children you lead?

ABOUT THE AUTHORS

BRENT COLBY

Brent Colby is a Seattle-born coffee drinker who develops leaders in the Northwest Ministry Network and at Northwest University. He has an amazing wife and three kids. He loves Jesus and loves to talk about leadership and culture at brentcolby.com.

brentcolby.com

ANNIE BAILEY

Annie has an MA in Professional Coaching from Assemblies of God Theological Seminary and is a credentialed minister. Her goal is to help pastors, churches, and business leaders better understand Millenials. She enjoys traveling, Middle Eastern food, and well-told stories.

facebook.com/anniebaileycoaching

MONICA BOWSHER

Monica Bowsher graduated from the University of Washington in 2011 and married her husband, James, in 2012. Together they serve on the leadership team at Newhope Church. Monica has a passion to see people come to know and grow in their relationship with Jesus.

facebook.com/monica.bowsher

NICK CAALIM

Nick and Stacy, married since 2003, are raising four boys in Lakewood. They have served at Life Center in Pierce County since 2002. In their free time...let's be honest, they are raising four buys boys... there is no free time. But you could usually find them talking about Pixar movies or Mariners baseball.

twitter.com/nickacaalim

JESSICA DOWNS

Jessica Downs graduated from Northwest University where she studied children's ministry and missions. She has been a children's pastor since 2010. She has a passion to reach out to children and families and present the life-changing message of Jesus in fun and interesting ways.

twitter.com/MrsDowns11

DORENE HEETER

Dorene is a veteran children's pastor as well as a gifted mentor and coach. She has served countless men and women as they discover their call to ministry. Missions has always been a driving passion for Dorene.

facebook.com/dorene.heeter

AMY JOHNSON

Amy Johnson became the children's pastor at Belfair Assembly in 2003. She has incredible energy and a passion for connecting children to Jesus. Her and her husband, Rob, have three children.

facebook.com/amy.s.johnson.52

DAN METTEER

Dan Metteer is a campus pastor who loves ultimate frisbee and disc golf. He loves children's ministry because he has a passion to see the next generation take seriously God's call on their lives. Dan is married with three kids.

twitter.com/danmetteer

BRYAN REEDER

Bryan Reeder has close to 15 years of pastoral experience. He earned his BA in Church Ministries from Southwestern Assemblies of God University and is licensed with the Assemblies of God. Bryan and Jalita have been married for 15 years, and they have three kids: Isaac, Austin, and Emma.

bryankreeder.blogspot.com

CHANTEL ROHR

Chantel Rohr grew up in Everett, Washington. She attended Northwest University where she met her husband, Brad, and graduated with a BA in Elementary Education. She became a children's pastor in Lacey, Washington until her first son, David was born. They also have a second son, Noah.

facebook.com/bradandchantel.rohr

KATE THAETE

Kate Thaete is the Family Ministries Pastor at Creekside Church in Mountlake Terrace, Washington. She has a passion for kids and gift for writing. Few leaders share Kate's ability to simplify and express complex ideas in simple ways.

facebook.com/Kate.thaete

WORKS CITED

Baker, Fiona. "Learning Styles in Children." *Kidspot.com* (http://www.kidspot.com.au/school/primary/learning-and-behaviour/learning-styles-in-children)

Barna, George. *Revolution*. Carol Stream, Ilinois: Tyndale Momentum, 2012.

Barna . "What Millennials Want When They Visit Church." *What Millennials Want When They Visit Church*, March 3, 2015. (https://www.barna.org/barna-update/millennials/711-what-millennials-want-when-they-visit-church#.VTmBia1Viko)

Barna, George, and Bill Hybels. *Transforming Children into Spiritual Champions*. Grand Rapids, Mich.: Baker Books, 2003.

Barseghian, Tina, and Jessica Kelmon. "Secrets to Raising Smart Kids: Determine Learning Style." *BabyCenter*. (http://www.babycenter.com/0_secrets-to-raising-smart-kids-determine-learning-style_10336240.bc)

Batterson, Mark. *In a Pit with a Lion on a Snowy Day: How to Survive and Thrive When Opportunity Roars*. Sisters, Ore.: Multnomah Books, 2006.

Berryman, Jerome. *Godly Play*. Minneapolis: Augsburg Books, 1995.

Blasi, Anna, Evelyne Mercure, Sarah Lloyd-Fox, et al. "Early Specialization for Voice and Emotion Processing in the Infant Brain." *Current Biology* 21, no. 14 (July 2011): 1220–24. doi:10.1016/j.cub.2011.06.009.

Brown, Sheldon. "Tandem Bicycles." Cycling Blog. *Harris Cyclery*. (http://www.sheldonbrown.com/tandem.html)

Cahalan, Susannah. "This Kid's a Text Maniac." *New York Post*, January 11, 2009. (http://nypost.com/2009/01/11/this-kids-a-text-maniac/)

Carr, Nicholas. *The Shallows: What the Internet Is Doing to Our Brains*. New York: W.W. Norton & Company, 2011.

Carr, Nicholas, and Jeff Cummings. *The Glass Cage: Automation and Us*. Brilliance Audio, 2014.

Chua, Celestine. "How to Give Constructive Criticism: 6 Helpful Tips." *Personal Excellence*. (http://personalexcellence.co/blog/constructive-criticism/)

Covey, Stephen R. *Principle-Centered Leadership*. New York: Fireside Press, 1992.

Crouch, Andy. *Culture Making: Recovering Our Creative Calling*. Downers Grove, Ill: IVP Books, 2008.

Detrick, Don. *Growing Disciples Organically: The Jesus Method of Spiritual Formation*. Sisters, Ore.: Deep River Books, 2013.

Diamandis, Peter H., and Steven Kotler. *Bold: How to Go Big, Create Wealth and Impact the World*. New York: Simon & Schuster, 2015.

Doidge, Norman. *The Brain That Changes Itself: Stories of Personal Triumph from the Frontiers of Brain Science*. New York: Viking, 2007.

Dyer, John, and T. David Gordon. *From the Garden to the City: The Redeeming and Corrupting Power of Technology*. Grand Rapids, Mich.: Kregel Publications, 2011.

Elmore, Tim, and Dan Cathy. *Generation iY: Our Last Chance to Save Their Future*. Atlanta, Ga.: Poet Gardener Publishing, 2010.

"Fetal Development: 1st Trimester." (http://www.mayoclinic.org/healthy-lifestyle/pregnancy-week-by-week/in-depth/prenatal-care/art-20045302)

Gardner, Howard E. *Multiple Intelligences: New Horizons in Theory and Practice*. New York: Basic Books, 2006.

Gladwell, Malcolm. *David and Goliath: Underdogs, Misfits, and the Art of Battling Giants*. New York: Little, Brown and Company, 2013.

Gruber, Dick. "[Podcast] Partnering with Parents, Internships | DickGruber.com." (http://www.dickgruber.com/podcast-partnering-with-parents-internships/)

Gunelius, Susan. "The Data Explosion in 2014 Minute by Minute—Infographic." *ACI*. (http://aci.info/2014/07/12/the-data-explosion-in-2014-minute-by-minute-infographic/)

Haynes, Brian. *Shift: What It Takes to Finally Reach Families Today*. Loveland, Colo.: Group Publishing, 2009.

Heath, Chip, and Dan Heath. *Made to Stick: Why Some Ideas Survive and Others Die*. New York: Random House, 2007.

Hendricks, Howard. *Teaching to Change Lives: Seven Proven Ways to Make Your Teaching Come Alive*. Sisters, Ore.: Multnomah Books, 2003.

Iran-Nejad, Asghar, and Sally Ann Zengaro. "Opportunity Prioritization, Biofunctional Simultaneity, and Psychological Mutual Exclusion." *Behavioral and Brain Sciences* 36, no. 6 (December 2013): 696–97; discussion 707–26. doi:http://dx.doi.org.seu.idm.oclc.org/10.1017/S0140525X13001088.

Joiner, Reggie. *Think Orange: Imagine the Impact When Church and Family Collide...* Colorado Springs: David C. Cook, 2009.

Joiner, Reggie, and Kristen Ivy. *It's Just a Phase—So Don't Miss It: Why Every Life Stage of a Kid Matters and at Least 13 Things Your Church Should Do About It*. Cumming, Ga.: Orange, a division of The reThink Group, 2015.

Keller, Gary, and Jay Papasan. *The ONE Thing: The Surprisingly Simple Truth Behind Extraordinary Results*. Austin, Tex.: Bard Press, 2013.

Kimmel, Tim. *Connecting Church & Home*. Nashville: Randall House, 2013.

Leman, Dr Kevin. *Making Children Mind without Losing Yours*. Grand Rapids, Mich.: Revell, 2005.

Lencioni, Patrick. *Getting Naked: A Business Fable About Shedding The Three Fears That Sabotage Client Loyalty*. San Francisco, Calif.: Jossey-Bass, 2010.

Lencioni, Patrick M. *The Advantage: Why Organizational Health Trumps Everything Else In Business*. San Francisco: Jossey-Bass, 2012.

Linsky, Martin, and Ronald A. Heifetz. *Leadership on the Line: Staying Alive through the Dangers of Leading*. Boston, Mass: Harvard Business Review Press, 2002.

Lyons, Gabe. *The Next Christians: The Good News About the End of Christian America*. New York: Doubleday Religion, 2010.

Mampe, Birgit, Angela D. Friederici, Anne Christophe, and Kathleen Wermke. "Newborns' Cry Melody Is Shaped by Their Native Language." *Current Biology* 19, no. 23 (December 2009): 1994–97. doi:10.1016/j.cub.2009.09.064.

Markos, Louis A. "Belonging Before Believing." *ChristianityToday.com*. (http://www.christianitytoday.com/ct/2007/february/43.124.html)

Maxwell, John C. *The 21 Irrefutable Laws of Leadership: Follow Them and People Will Follow You*. Nashville: Thomas Nelson, 2007.

McKeown, Greg. *Essentialism: The Disciplined Pursuit of Less*. New York: Crown Business, 2014.

Newberg, Andrew, and Mark Robert Waldman. *How God Changes Your Brain: Breakthrough Findings from a Leading Neuroscientist*. New York: Ballantine Books, 2009.

Parsley, Ross. *Messy Church: A Multigenerational Mission for God's Family*. Colorado Springs: David C. Cook, 2012.

Pew Research. "Millennials: A Portrait of Generation Next." Pew Research Center, February 2010. (http://www.pewsocialtrends.org/files/2010/10/millennials-confident-connected-open-to-change.pdf)

Pew Research Center. "Millennials in Adulthood." *Pew Research Center's Social & Demographic Trends Project*. (http://www.pewsocialtrends.org/2014/03/07/millennials-in-adulthood/)

Powell, Kara E., Chap Clark, John Ortberg, and Jim Candy. *Sticky Faith: Everyday Ideas to Build Lasting Faith in Your Kids*. Grand Rapids, Mich: Zondervan, 2011.

Raphelson, Samantha. "Amid The Stereotypes, Some Facts About Millennials." *NPR.org*. (http://www.npr.org/2014/11/18/354196302/amid-the-stereotypes-some-facts-about-millennials)

Rath, Tom, and Barry Conchie. *Strengths Based Leadership: Great Leaders, Teams, and Why People Follow*. New York: Gallup Press, 2008.

Searcy, Nelson, and Jennifer Dykes Henson. *Connect: How to Double Your Number of Volunteers*. Grand Rapids, Mich.: Baker Books, 2012.

Senge, Peter M. *The Fifth Discipline: The Art and Practice of the Learning Organization*. New York: Doubleday/Currency, 2006.

Sinek, Simon. *Start with Why: How Great Leaders Inspire Everyone to Take Action*. New York: Portfolio, 2011.

Smith, Christian, Kari Christoffersen, Hilary Davidson, and Patricia Snell Herzog. *Lost in Transition: The Dark Side of Emerging Adulthood*. New York: Oxford University Press, 2011.

Sousa, David A. *How the Brain Learns*. Thousand Oaks, Calif: Corwin, 2011.

Stanley, Andy. *Next Generation Leader: 5 Essentials for Those Who Will Shape the Future*. Sisters, Ore.: Multnomah Books, 2006.

Stanley, Andy, and Lane Jones. *Communicating for a Change: Seven Keys to Irresistible Communication*. Sisters, Ore.: Multnomah Books, 2006.

St. Clair, Chantelle. "Disengaging From Stereotypes: Evolution of Entrepreneurs." *LinkedIn Pulse*. (https://www.linkedin.com/pulse/disengaging-from-stereotypes-evolution-entrepreneurs-st-clair)

Tobias, Cynthia Ulrich. *The Way They Learn*. Carol Stream, Ill.: Focus on the Family, 1998.

Toyama, Kentaro. *Geek Heresy: Rescuing Social Change from the Cult of Technology*. New York: PublicAffairs, 2015.

Tripp, Tedd. *Shepherding a Child's Heart*. Wapwallopen, Penn.: Shepherd Press, 1995.

I using, Keith. "Creating the Annual Ministry Calendar." *Cmbuzx.com*, November 17, 2015. (http://cmbuzz.com/2011/10/planning-the-childrens-ministry-annual-calendar/)

Tyson, Jon, and Barna Group. *Sacred Roots: Why the Church Still Matters*. Grand Rapids, Mich.: Zondervan, 2014.

"Visual, Auditory and Kinesthetic (VAK) Learning Style Model." (http://www.jcu.edu.au/wiledpack/modules/fsl/JCU_090460.html)

Vogt, Brandon. *The Church and New Media: Blogging Converts, Online Activists, and Bishops Who Tweet*. Huntington, Ind: Our Sunday Visitor, 2011.

Williams, Roy H., and Michael R. Drew. *Pendulum: How Past Generations Shape Our Present and Predict Our Future*. New York: Vanguard Press, 2012.

Yount Jones, Christine. "Exclusive Research: The State of Family Ministry." *Children's Ministry*. (http://childrensministry.com/articles/exclusive-research-state-family-ministry/)

Zarrella, Dan. *Zarrella's Hierarchy of Contagiousness: The Science, Design, and Engineering of Contagious Ideas*. Amazon/Do You Zoom. The Domino Project, 2011.